THE PARTY CONTINUES

Dick Z. Lenn

ISBN 978-1-953223-40-1 (paperback)
ISBN 978-1-953223-39-5 (digital)

Copyright © 2020 by Dick Z. Lenn

All rights reserved. No part of this publication may be reproduced, distributed, or transmitted in any form or by any means, including photocopying, recording, or other electronic or mechanical methods without the prior written permission of the publisher. For permission requests, solicit the publisher via the address below.

Rushmore Press LLC
1 800 460 9188
www.rushmorepress.com

Printed in the United States of America

Brandy awoke in a cold sweat dammit after all of these years she still could see Chloe in the blood bath the pain was so real she could recall the very ache she felt in her heart she felt it right now piercing through her heart like a knife blade she could to this day recall every detail that night. Was it because Chloe was her first love or because it was the first dead body she ever witnessed she didn't know one thing she did know was that to this day that night still haunted her fueled her drive to make sure she got scum of the streets. Every detail about the case was on her mind she had entered the academy with Chloe and a few other girls. They had the idea to conquer the academy. She smiled at the memory of how brazen they were clear creek was their dream. They wanted to leave their mark on that academy and save lives that was the part that got to her the most why did it have to be she saved lives but the one life that mattered the most to her was the one that she failed. Brandy wiped the tears as she lit a cig she didn't smoke but kept a pack around for moments like this. She stood, looked out the window, she still could see that smile for most of her teenage life that smile was what prompted her to go to school hell it prompted her to become the lead detective she was today. She took a slow drag of the cigarette secretly hoping it would somehow wipe away the pain. Most of all she could still smell a hint of that musky perfume Chloe would spray on her before they would go out. Oh what she would give to just have one more moment with her. Why did life have to throw curves why did Chloe have to die so needlessly. Brandy met Chloe in high school they hit it off almost immediately Brandy smiled as she recalled their first encounter she would never forget Chloe's face after the old lady called the principal out Brandy was shy back then when it came to females. Chloe had spoken frankly *'Damn she got balls!' 'she is mad' 'I can see that doll face just never saw anyone stand up to Grizzly Adams before'* Brandy inhaled as she took another drag of her cigarette she heard the knock saw Maria come in. Brandy closed her eyes she didn't want to wake her

> "You ok? I smelled the cigarette."

Brandy ran her hand over her face as she spoke in a shaky voice

> "I'll be ok mar"

Brandy could tell by the look on the woman face that she didn't buy that line for a second

> "Come on Brandy talk to me"

Brandy didn't know if it was the way she said it or if it was because she saw the pain mirrored in the woman's eyes either way she knew she was toast so she sighed

> "Fine"

Brandy sat down knowing Maria wouldn't leave until she was satisfied and since Brandy needed it off of her chest she placed her elbows on her knees she looked into the woman's eyes as she began

> "I've never told anyone this story the only people who know are the people that were with me at that time mar"

she wanted to stress that this wasn't something that was going to be easy for her to talk about and she knew that Maria would understand because like Brandy Maria did suffer a big loss as well

> "Anybody?"

Maria heard the word come out of her mouth she was floored she didn't know why she knew Brandy was a private person she knew she had her crew she kept close and if they didn't know then that meant that it had to be something that Brandy herself was struggling with. Well Maria took a deep breath she would do the best she could

> "No only three people know that's only because they knew me and where with me that night"

Maria could see the pain all over Brandy's face at this point she didn't know what to do she had never saw Brandy so lost

> "Really well you look like hell Brandy maybe I can help?"

Brandy looked in her eyes as she began suddenly she felt the weight of all of those years creep up on her but she continued she wanted this at least manageable instead of dealing with it after every case it seemed like she closed her eyes,

> "I met this girl in high school she just so happened to be in the office at the same time I was. We hit it off, she was the sunshine in my life Maria she was the reason I became who I am today the woman meant everything to me she was wonderful brilliant funny and highly frustrating at times. We both wanted the same things outta life you know family and to save lives we were at the academy together. We wanted to leave our mark there come here and be the best we could be by saving people. Well one day she got called to the captains office we didn't think nothing of it because she often times had odd jobs to do in the office. She was the secretary or something like that she told me one time she wanted to know the whole layout be able to do anything that way when she came out she would be able to get a job anywhere and work her way up. The others and I were in drills that day we busted ass from sun up to sunset. We didn't think nothing of it when we finished the drills and she wasn't back because sometimes she would work late. She wanted her resume pristine but as

the hours grew we knew something was wrong. She wouldn't stay out and chance a mark against her so me and the girls we went searching for her car that was when we found the cops and the bloodbath they fucking mutilated her. She was the most amazing thing in my life and they fucking tore her up took me awhile to get back to it. They gave us time off if it wasn't for Gwen I don't know what I would have done so now after almost every case I get hit with flashbacks of that night just like your love was taken away from you mine was taken away from me and just like you it was tragically. How does your heart overcome something like that?"

Maria looked at the one woman who had become her life sure she had Adicus but he was off doing his shoots and Katie was in Kentucky so Brandy vastly became her life her heart ached as she watched the tears roll down Brandy's cheeks then she spoke

"I don't think the heart ever recovers from the loss of a loved one. I think we as human beings just learn how to live with it from day to day. Did you catch who did it?"

Brandy looked in her eyes and Maria could tell that at that moment Brandy was truly listening

"Yeah they did that's why I dedicate my life to what I do every day for her."

Maria could tell she was reeling so she found her opening and spoke up

"I'm sure she would want you to be happy too Brandy"

Maria watched as the light came back for a brief second but then leave again she heard her speak as she lit another cigarette

"Haven't found one that fits the bill yet Mar"

Maria did know one thing and she would make sure she got her point across. She had pined for Sophia for so long that before she knew it 20 years had flew by she would not let that happen to Brandy

> "You will"

> "You didn't"

That simple response stunned Maria. She wasn't looking for it and she couldn't deny the sting from the brutal truth and she knew now was the time to lay it all out.

> "That's my fault I tried to hang on to Soph but listen to me Brandy one thing I do know is you can't let this hold you up. I'm not saying forget her all. I'm saying is allow yourself to live."

She could tell that the thought brought more pain but Maria knew one thing she knew that now was the time for Brandy to hear this and she wished to god she had someone back then to tell her the same thing. She probably wouldn't be lonely at nights

> "I don't know Mar I'll try. I'm ok just nights like tonight first time back you know it really hits me hard"

She sighed as she sat beside Brandy on the recliner she took her hand looked her in the eyes

> "Look I know it is going to be painful but trust me you will thank me later. Sure I loved Sophia I still do but I would do anything to have someone give me advice on what to do with so much grief. It's kind of like throwing your life away if you don't do anything and I know that is not what Chloe would want for you."

Brandy put her cigarette out and stood she folded her arms and spoke

> "I know she wouldn't. She would definitely kick my ass if I throw my life away. I know what you say is

true Maria but dammit sometimes the truth hurts you know."

Maria smiled as Brandy gave her a hug and went to the door in satisfaction knowing that Brandy was going to be ok. She heard Brandy say

"Thanks Maria a lot!"

"Anytime"

Brandy sat at her desk she had a plaque made it was in honor of Chloe it was a way for her to still have a part of Chloe with her and she still could move on. Her talk with Maria really helped maybe all she really needed to do was just let it out. She didn't know all she knew was she was back and ready for business though when she looked at the file on her desk and saw the name Big Amigos she knew that her next job was going to be a big one. One that she knew would take everything she had and then some but she knew that every time she put her uniform on she was saving lives she looked at her plaque before she stood it only held a quote but a quote that she lived by *'saving lives is more than my job it's my heartbeat'* she knew the Big Amigos was her current objective. She knew that to keep the streets safe she needed to grab the monster by the horns still every once in a while she let her mind wonder in the what if department but she knew as long as she grinded and did her best she was doing what Chloe would want her too she did wonder what it would be like working with Chloe but she didn't too much though. Baxter came in he saw the look he knew Brandy enough to know that the look on her face right now meant she had something on her mind and was far away so he had to ask just too make sure she was good

"You good blondie?"

He saw her look at him and smile when he saw the smile and the light in her eyes he knew that his lead detective was fine and that sure made the worry ease off of his shoulders. Brandy was his best man and he need her 100 percent he heard her answer,

"Fine"

He wanted to make sure he knew she was secretive but he also knew that whatever it was it was something that hurt her so he asked,

"You sure?"

Brandy knew he was being serious she also knew that he probably could pin it down in five minutes and she didn't want to have to answer questions so she stood and truth be told she was fine so she sighed cleared her throat as she came around the desk and to him,

"I'm good captain!"

She saw the relief wash over him she knew he cared and that meant a lot right now. What she wanted to do was focus on the gang that was tearing up the town and bring them to justice

"Good."

Brandy smiled as she accepted the hugs from her team. At last the brutal assignment had come to an end. At last another infamous drug dealer had gone down and was out of society. She watched as the cruiser drove off, she shook her head knowing that even though she nailed one there still were plenty more out there. Her team was after the top bastard and even though he wasn't on the top she knew he was on the totem pole. She watched as Baxter walked her way suddenly, she felt the whole four months on her shoulders

"So blonde good collar"

Brandy locked eyes with Baxter she knew he wouldn't let her question the scuzz bag. Oh but how she wanted too she needed to know what he knew she had questions that needed answered it was times like this that she truly didn't like the job. She knew Gwen and Bax would do their job still she had the insight she had the knowledge which sometimes was too much to bare she smirked,

"For now, yes it was a small victory!"

Baxter shook his head and smiled he knew Brandy well enough to know she wasn't going to be happy until they had all the bastards locked up, honestly he wasn't either the Big Amigos have terrorized the southern Cal area long enough and he wouldn't rest until every last one was where they belonged he spoke,

"Ready to go home?"

Brandy never thought she would be so glad to hear those words

He watched the blonde look into his eyes he saw the fire flash in her eyes he knew if that look could speak it would speak a multitude of words

"Not until he tells us where Bradford is!"

Bax held back the smile Brandy wouldn't be Brandy without a protest.

"Trust me he will but you can't intervene not yet!"

Baxter folded his arms as he got ready for the line he knew was coming,

"Look I have a lot of blood and sweat not to mention time into this. I'm not stepping aside."

"No, your saving face. He has connections you'll be made in nothing flat."

Baxter countered at that moment. Baxter looked into her eyes and knew that she had to see something to give this much trouble.

Brandy hated not being the one who gets to grill the scuzz bag but she knew Baxter was correct if she went in there, she knew she couldn't go under and that would be a loss on her end. So, she sighed turned around and put her hands behind her back she closed her eyes as she spoke

"Fine let's do this then."

He knew Gwen would ask about Brandy even though they weren't blood family they were inseparable Baxter felt like he was now a part of that like a domineering big brother or something Baxter placed the cuffs on her hands. He led her to the awaiting cruiser. He figured Brandy would be a bigger handful than that with the wipe of his brow he closed the door. He then let the breath release as he watched Gwen walk his way. She was exactly 5'0 and could use every inch of it too. He remembered when he was first signed her partner his worst mistake was underestimating the height, she had him in a choke hold in 5 flat then told him a thing or two. They since then have covered each other's backs for going on eight years and Baxter couldn't ask for a better partner. Gwen looked at the clipboard not noticing Baxter's lost look Gwen walked up to Baxter she watched as he cleared his throat,

"Did she say anything?"

Baxter shot out an exasperating breath as he ran a hand through his hair as he answered,

"Nothing other than Bradford is still in business."

They both knew that meant the Big Amigos were just getting started up until now they were just committing petty crimes but both knew with Bradford running loose things were just heating up.

Gwen did look up and meet Baxter's eyes,

"We'll get him!"

They both knew that was more spoken in hope of sooner rather than later.

They arrived at the precinct. Baxter never was so glad to let the blonde out. He could swear he still could hear her badgering him he smiled as he watched her head towards the showers he found Gwen,

"Did you call pap?"

"Yup"

Baxter smiled as Gwen sipped her coffee,

"Well?"

"He has a job for her that will keep her busy long enough for us to locate Bradford and figure out our next move."

Gwen could see the wheels turning in Baxter's face she smiled as he nodded.

"Good she needs a break and honestly so do we."

Gwen found Brandy at the coffee pot pouring herself some stale cup java. She had cleaned up and was dressed in her uniform. Gwen cleared her throat knowing Brandy. She would want to dive right in,

"So, what's the plan?"

Gwen silently chuckled as Brandy was always nothing but business that was why she was so glad that pap had called. Brandy needed a break and pap had provided one. Pap was Brandy's uncle but he was more like a grandfather well hers too. He was a clever old man who knew just how to get what he wanted and he would have it before you could realize just what he had done. Gwen sighed as she poured herself some coffee.

"Gramps called wants you to go see him."

Brandy shot Gwen a suspicious look

"Why?"

Gwen should have known she would think it was about paps failing health. They got the news about the Big C a couple months ago and even though pap was optimistic about it. They both had seen the effect on him almost immediately she spoke,

"I don't know said he had some detective work for you to do for him. Said it would be a big favor since his old bones didn't work like yours did."

THE PARTY CONTINUES

Brandy leaned against the counter she was a busty blonde with a slim waist to look at her one would definitely want to go there men had tried and left packing their hearts and their pride. Gwen knew Brandy was saving herself for someone great. She was there that night that Chloe was killed she never saw Brandy so hurt and pissed at the same time she knew that was a changing point in Brandy's life Gwen smiled as she folded her arms,

"Detective work?"

"Seemed urgent."

"Fine since to how you all won't let me do anything here anyway besides I need to check on pap anyway."

Gwen watched her head towards the door,

"Love you cuz!"

She watched Brandy wave her off and walk out the door Gwen chuckled!

George D Hawke was an eighty-five-year-old man who had seen a lot of things in his life. He was known for his cleverness as well as his cunning ability to get what he wants. Hell, that's how he landed the Flames franchise. He sat in a poker game ready to call when the frisky young man threw in everything. George still smiles about that night. He had his eye on a point guard. The team needed a shake up and the young chap had game. Plus he knew his niece could use this time to maybe explore and see if she found something that might put more meaning back into her life. Sure he knew she loved Chloe and as a man who lost his wife he knew you had to move on so this trip was for his point guard. Sure but just maybe it would be more than just a scouting job. He knew his niece would come in all heated, especially with her coming off a stint and especially with Baxter and Gwen not letting her inquire, he knew she would be in fits. Another reason he hoped she would explore the bluegrass state and hopefully find someone she could get to know and maybe have a little fun. Get a little steam off! He chuckled at the thought of her response.

He smiled as he heard her voice outside his door. He sat down ready to get to work to make sure by the end of the week he had Melanie Brooks. That was his argument anyway. She came in a full head of steam just as he had expected he watched as his niece walked in full force. He couldn't help but bite back the chuckle even though Brandy wasn't blood, his sister's child. She ran through her so purely like now arms folded chin stuck out just like his sister's boy could he tell stories about that very look he remembered the very day that she brought Brandy home, a feisty little blonde headed kid, who was so scared he knew that she would work out the kinks and turn her into a wonderful woman and she had now. He knew he had to step up and help her while she was hurting only he wasn't going to tell. her he did it until he knew she was hooked for life. He heard her speak, he ran a hand over his greying beard he stood put his hands in his pockets started around his desk

> "Ok Gramps what's going on?"

He cleared his throat as he leaned against his desk a move he did when he was setting a plan into motion he watched as she put her hands into her pockets

> "How do you like cold weather?'

He watched as he saw the confused look on her face he figured he would start off easy

> "Hate it?"

He folded his arms as he spoke.

> "Better get to loving it doll I need you to scout for me!"

He watched the information process the questions start coming out of her mouth

> "Scout? I just got back. Besides I haven't scouted in years Gramps,"

He chuckled as he knew he had her. He told Gwen and Baxter he would keep her busy and he would so he played his ace in the hole

> "I know it's perfect because I know you have your to go bag you always have a to go bag as well as those keys. Besides Baxter said you could use some fresh air. I also think you need fresh air take this opportunity Brandy and go not just because I need this point guard although I desperately need this point guard but take this time and just take time for you. Of course after you get me my point guard."

He watched as she let the information process she stood ran a hand over her face and gave in. He went back around the desk and sat down in his chair, she could tell he was pale, it was from the chemo and the radiation and it wouldn't do any good to ask him. He would just play it off and avoid the subject, she spoke

> "Fine where am I going?"

He handed her the file knowing that Brandy would be sold on the numbers he watched as Brandy saw the statistics and arc a brow she locked eyes with him. He smiled,

> "The Bluegrass State? The point guard plays for the University of Kentucky Wildcats. Her name is Red Hot, just what I need to turn this franchise into a winning machine. She is a total phenomenon and rocked high school nearly tripled her averages in college. I want that acceptance letter in my hand by the end of the week. I want her before Bruce has a chance at her."

She never wanted to go to the bluegrass state but she had to admit her curiosity was raging from the statistics she was looking at these numbers and they were rare and that meant the player was as well. He intentionally left the picture out of the file knowing his niece he knew she would have fun in that area and he hoped that she would.

She needed it too but first and foremost he needed his point guard then she could use the distraction. He knew about Chloe about how brutally she was taken from his niece that had rage burning in his chest he will never forget the look of defeat in her eyes and that blank expression she carried everywhere she went. He was secretly hoping that this trip would do more than land him a point guard he was hoping it would liven his niece up and bring her out she needed that,

"You know I hate cold weather pap!"

She sputtered as she sat in the chair she watched him push it off and state,

"Wear a jacket and go get me my number one!"

"Janell will be pissed!"

She was right Janel would be pissed but it was nothing that he couldn't handle and nothing that he wouldn't handle. He knew he would have it taken care of just sometimes you need to know the right people.

"I'll handle that just go get that letter for me!"

He shot her a look that had reminded her of the one lady that taught her everything she knew. She knew that was a look of no bullshit that look meant she was going whether she wanted to or not and she would do what he said or else she knew he was none too good to whoop her ass at his age and she wouldn't let it come to that,

"I'll see what I can do!"

she stood sighed knowing now she didn't have a choice but to see what Kentucky held for her she started for the door telling herself the positives of this trip could be many,

"I'll call the jet."

"No I'll drive I need the time to myself!"

"Okay remember!"

Brandy smiled as she went to the door and she looked into the aging man's eyes and gave him that earnest look she knew she wasn't keen on the idea but she also knew when she does a job she gives one hundred and ten percent so she smiled,

"Gramps I got this."

"That's my girl."

That's what he was looking for now. He knew that his plan was in action and he knew that she would do everything in her power to get him, Melanie Brooks, he need that point guard he wanted to at least have one ring before he kicked the bucket. Oh hell he knew he could get more than one with her on his roster. He chuckled, as he lit a cigar as he celebrated his small victory now if his plan worked for both that would be the huge victory!

Brandy didn't mind going to Kentucky. She hadn't had the pleasure of seeing the bluegrass state getting to meet a chick on top of that hell, *priceless!* She smiled as she headed east she loved road trips the time she had to herself especially after a grueling 4 months stint she knew that she'd have to go under to nail Bradford. She wanted to make sure that collar didn't have anything to do with glory. She just wanted to nail the bastard. She saw firsthand just how much of a sick bastard he was. No young adult was safe with him out and about. She just hoped that with Henry caught he might stay quiet for a while. Henry was on the totem pole. She knew he was. She also knew Henry wouldn't talk, not without reassurances. She still was pissed that Bax and Gwen wouldn't let her have at him. She couldn't tell them what she had saw what she had witnessed she couldn't tell them anything. She gripped the steering wheel so tight her knuckles grew white, the shrill of the cell phone brought her out of thought. She rolled her eyes as she saw Shelly's number. She heard that sunny voice still didn't help her dark mood,

"What?" she felt bad that she came out a little harsher than she should have.

"Where are you? Gwen said you grabbed another job."

Damn Gwen for telling her anything she didn't want anyone knowing where she was. Why it is that common courtesy was hard to come by.

"Well I have what's up?"

Brandy said in a short tone, she didn't have the patience to deal with her right now. Not after getting slammed with this trip not after she couldn't get the answers she needed from him, she sighed.

"We had a date that's what's up."

Brandy closed her eyes she totally forgot about that. She knew that the relationship was on the rocks but she just didn't have her heart in it and it didn't have anything to do with Chloe either. She just did not feel like they were meant to be together,

"Look, I have to do some detective work for Gramps."

Brandy let out an exasperating breath she just wanted the conversation over with.

"How long will that be?"

"I don't know!"

Brandy seriously wanted to throw her phone at that moment.

"Fine I'll wait. Just know I want you"

"Do you now?"

"Yes, I do?"

"I'll let you know when I know."

Brandy did sigh as she guided the car down the freeway she decided to be nice it wasn't her fault she didn't have anything to do with what had happened today or the fact that she was in a piss poor mood.

"Ok baby?"

"Okay."

Brandy sighed she didn't even know why she agreed to date Shelley, sure she was great just not exactly what Brandy wanted. She knew she loved the job and Shelley had been great with that but something was amiss

Melanie Brooks stepped out of her Honda Civic. She didn't like to think of herself as anything more than a teammate. She grabbed her bag as Cyn climbed out. Melanie was a 5'8" brunette she was built with a petite body. She had piercing blue eyes that stopped anyone who got a glance. She looked at Cyn with a stern look. She watched as the blonde pleaded her case about the party at her place. Melanie did enjoy a good party but she didn't especially when they were in the middle of a championship run.

"Come on Mels"

"No I can't have any distractions you heard, coach.
After Paula-

Melanie shook her head. She had put everything into her career nothing was getting in the way of that nothing.

"I know but this is different."

Melanie shook her head. Cyn was a wonderful friend the best but man the chick sometimes just did not listen she told her again,

"Look I love ya' but ball is my way out."

Cyn looked Melanie's way she knew she was all about ball but she felt it was her duty as a friend to see that she got out. Yeah she knew the orange was Melanie's way out. She also knew she would never do anything to fuck that up so she just said,

"Okay"

Melanie headed to the gym C watched the Audi pull in she let out a whistle sure Audi's were everywhere and yes they were a normal sight but this Audi was different it glistened and shined plus this particular Audi was different it was new and sleek. Melanie turned to see the sleek german machine pull into the parking lot she rolled her eyes all she wanted to do was get this game over and done with Cyn smiled as she spoke,

"Ooh smooth ride."

Melanie rolled her eyes unamused by the car she turned and started back to the gym Cyn hurried to catch her

"Yeah probably a booster come on!"

Brandy climbed out so here was the Rupp Arena. She had heard about the place but didn't know the first thing about where to go and who to see she scanned the parking lot where she found two ladies who happened to be carrying their gym bags. She needed to be pointed in the right direction. She saw the girls head to the building hell she didn't know where to start but she did see them holding game gear and heading to the players entrance so she decided she had to start somewhere so she spoke up,

"Hey!"

She watched the brunette turn around. In that instance she was slammed with the effect of those blue eyes just that charge alone left Brandy breathless she couldn't think about anything all she could think was damn. Brandy was still reeling from the affect when she heard the blonde speak. Melanie felt her oxygen level plummet. Booster or not she totally wrecked her world in an instant. C spoke

"Can we help you?"

Cyn folded her arms as she sized up the busty blonde which wasn't hard since to. How the woman held an hour glass shape and there was plenty to look at. She looked like she jumped out of a fashion magazine. Melanie stole a glance as well. She knew this woman was not from Kentucky. She could not explain how she knew but she knew,

"I'm looking for a Melanie Brooks"

Melanie felt the lump in her throat as she heard her name come from those inviting lips. She heard Cyn ask

"What do you want with her?"

It was at that moment she found the one thing that could distract her. The one thing that could throw her off her game. The very object she would so want to spend time with. She knew she could not let it show so she hid the effect as the blonde asked,

"Just to talk."

Melanie felt the blush rise on her cheeks. Why did a broad like that want to talk to her? She had to admit curiosity had her so wanting to just say ok and have those brown eyes on her for however long the discussion took place but most usually broads like that were involved with the press and that was one group of people she hated to deal with. Sure, she knew she had to mean she liked it. She smirked and asked,

"What do you want?"

Melanie watched as those brown eyes landed squarely on her. Brandy felt her body vibrate. It was at that moment she knew gramps had set her up. Just by that one question Brandy's world was upside down. She cursed under her breath. How was she to concentrate on getting a contract on watching her play when all she wanted to do was kiss her so she gathered what whit she had left and asked,

"Are you Melanie Brooks?"

Melanie saw how she affected the woman. She had to smile, sure she was gay and didn't mind to show it but she knew with her being in the company of this woman. She would definitely be having fun. She never met anyone who rocked her world with just the lock of eyes and she sure as hell wasn't going to be easy to get rid of. She wasn't going to give the lady what she wanted just so she could leave. Hell no but to be sitting in front of this lady with the best set of breast she had ever seen and answering questions. Melanie sighed, she closed her eyes to Melanie that question seemed so hard to answer not because she didn't know the woman but because she was still trying to regain herself after the effect of meeting her. So she regained as much composure as she could. Brandy watched as the heat flashed in them blue eyes. Blue eyes that Brandy found herself heating up at the thought of them lips. She let her mind wonder in other areas as well. She knew now that gramps had intentionally left out the photo and he intentionally sent her here just because of this moment right here. She never felt her body vibrate so much. She cleared her throat as the brunette locked eyes with her. She arced a brow and replied

"Yes, I am and I'm running late for warm ups."

Brandy ran a hand through her hair. She had to smile. She knew she was playing hard to get. She knew she was being difficult. Brandy didn't mind the chase was going to be as fun as the moment, when she does actually get to sit down with her

> "Look I need to chat with you but it's cool. We will do this your way. Melanie I have all the time in the world. Just know that when I do catch you the effect is still going to be there!"

Melanie felt the heat rush through her so fast she almost gasped. She looked in the woman's eyes and saw amusement. Melanie cleared her throat,

THE PARTY CONTINUES

> "We have done nothing but chat. Please know while I will admit that you do affect me. I know that I affect you too so we can play this both ways chick. I have a game tonight if you want to talk to me so bad it'll have to be after that."

Brandy loved the spunk, another point on Brandy's checklist. This woman was on her list, both list personal and professional, she had never wanted a human the way she ached for the woman who stood in front of her right now. She spoke as she shrugged her shoulders. Brandy knew pap would be pissed if she didn't get Red Hot to commit and she would be so pissed to not at least get to make a play so she spoke,

> "Fine, I'll take what I can get. I hope your ready Melanie. I have a feeling I am going to rock your world!"

> "Sure of yourself ain't ya blondie?"

> "You can say that I'll be around. Melanie just reach out to me when you are ready to talk"

Melanie watched the blond climb back into the fancy German machine and drive off. She felt her body vibrate damn the blonde not even five minutes and she already had her frustrated. She smiled as she headed to the gym. She rolled her eyes as Cyn spoke

> "Damn she's hot!"

Melanie spoke quietly more so to herself than to her friend as she made her way to locker room. She got dressed for the game.

> "You have your eye on Sarah and yes I know"

> "You get to sit across from that! Damn I'm so jealous seems to me that you and blonde have a thing"

> "Oh Cyn stop! You know me, I am solo and will stay solo!"

She knew the minute it left her mouth it was a lie. She so wanted to have the blonde on her arm to be able to say hey that's my girl. She probably was taken. They always are when they come in a package like that. Melanie didn't want to admit it but she was excited she also knew she couldn't allow the blonde to distract her. Not in this game, it was the championship game and it was against Richter and Sal. She desperately needed to stay focused and stay on point. She had a score to settle and she would tonight. Suddenly she remembered why Joe told her to use the distraction to her advantage. That was just what she was going to do too. She smiled as she vaguely heard Cyn still rambling on about the hot blonde,

> "We don't even know why she is here wanting to talk to me. It's probably the damn press and I hate dealing with that shit!"

Melanie said as she was tying her shoes. Cyn smiled as she tapped her shoulder and blasted,

> "Girl she be no press that is a legit woman. I didn't see no press pass. We both know those goons have those damn cards around their necks."

"Trust me Cyn I know she is a legit woman."

"Oh somebody got the bug!"

"You can't tell me she wasn't sending hints out there?"

"I know she was. I just didn't know…"

"Never mind Cyn we got a game to win. I'll deal with all of this when I get done on the floor."

Melanie had to admit she didn't see a press pass. Hell she didn't even care when she was talking to her. She didn't seem like she was press. Hell she would have boomed with questions, personal questions, if she was right. Still she didn't know, she didn't even think she cared. All she could think about when it came to the blonde was those lips that body. Damn she heated up just thinking about her. She couldn't think about it as she stood. She replied,

> "I don't know, I guess I'll be finding out later. Now I need to get my reps in before the game."

Brandy found the arena called Rupp Arena she vastly learned from a brochure that she had acquired. The Rupp Arena was named after the one and only Adolf Rupp. She followed the flow of traffic to the women's basketball floor. She had to give the city of Lexington credit they may be small town but they sure did manage to show visitors that they can keep up. She smiled as she claimed her seat she noticed that most of the jerseys that the fans wore were number 13 when she located number 13 on the floor it was Melanie Brooks aka Red Hot. She felt the similar vibrations start as she let her eyes roam on that body. She smiled as she knew gramps would have her behind the bench. She also knew that the sneaky old man had to know how she would react to her. She found her seat then scanned the floor for the tall dark haired woman who literally stole her oxygen. Brandy never met anyone who affected her like that just from one meeting and not even a meeting just a brief discussion and she was a mess already wanting to have another conversation. Brandy smirked as she watched her hands shake how it could be just one glance at those piercing blue eyes. She was toast. She located the woman. She was shooting the tree with ease. Brandy was blew away by her accuracy. She mentally calculated the percentage which at the moment was 94%. Brandy was brought too by a chipper voice calling out to her name,

> "Hey!"

She saw the middle aged red head with dangling earrings and a broad smile. Brandy replied in a short tone not really wanting to chat. She was trying to calm herself down long enough to actually do her job,

> "Hey?"

Brandy locked eyes with the aging red headed coach. Who seemed excited beyond measure she heard her add,

"George said you'd be here."

Brandy focused on the brunette who had her attention both professionally and personally and one had nothing to do with the other. Brandy stated,

"Did he now?"

"Yeah said the flames are eager to see my Red Hot play!"

Brandy took a drink of her coke telling herself she was eager to do a lot of things with Melanie Brooks. She rolled her eyes but she didn't want anyone to know why she was here she just wanted to watch the game and come to her own conclusion and if her game was anything like the effect she had on her then she knew the flames would definitely be seeing a ring.

"That's the plan as I sat here I can see that the tree is the sweet spot since she's at 94%!"

Brandy knew her players she knew talent too that's why pap recruited her for her eye and knowledge of the game sometimes even Baxter and his woman Samantha call on her whitt to win the fantasy league. She smiled reminiscing about that she was brought to by the lady going on about Melanie she just wanted the lady to leave her be,

"OH honey that isn't nothing."

If one thing made Brandy mad it was coaches trying to get an inch ahead so she pulled out the old rough as nails bit hoping it would send her away?

"I know see the flames have the three we need the leadership and the mental clarity along with an inside game."

Brandy knew she was being tough but she also knew that if anyone was telling the gorgeous brunette that she was a flame it was going to be her. Even if it were to see those blue eyes again. Coach cleared her throat and at that instance knew exactly why George had sent the blonde. She smiled as she patted Brandy on the shoulder knowing that Melanie held every tool that the flames were looking for. She spoke,

> "Just sit back and enjoy the show. I have no doubt by the time you're done you'll be begging for her signature."

Brandy didn't need her to tell her that she already knew that she didn't intend on begging but she was not above it. She knew and highly hoped she would have Melanie eating out of her hand just as she knew that Melanie already had her doing the same but she simply replied

> "Well we'll see won't we!"

She breathed a sigh of relief as she was finally able to concentrate.

Brandy eagerly watched as Melanie took her spot on the floor she couldn't help but feel the tingle up her spine when those deep pools of blue landed on hers for a split second then she watched as the coach looked back her way one last time and winked. Melanie took the ball up the court and stutter stepped and made her charge to the basket and gave the ball to the blonde who laid it in. Brandy nodded in approval flashy but controlled they definitely needed that type of leadership.

By the time the first quarter was over Brandy had done cleared off the mental checklist for franchise and for herself. She had done determined Melanie Brooks was the key to them winning the championship. She watched as Melanie jogged back out onto the court she held all the qualities that they needed and then some on a personal level. Those eyes had her vibrating never had she been that affected by anyone.

Cyn jogged up next to Melanie she leaned into her,

"Blondie's here."

Melanie had been trying to block that fact out all night. Hell she knew when the woman walked in she caught those eyes as soon as she stepped on the floor. She didn't need the distraction and applied the one thing that Joe had told her repeatedly just to get through just as she had to now to stay focused. She was guarded by one of the best in the league and couldn't afford a fuck up so she simply brushed it off no matter how she felt inside she couldn't show it,

"So?"

"So? Man we all know why."

Cyn wasn't helping damn she so wasn't helping so she repeated the same scenario that had been repeated to her.

> "Look I can't get distracted ok if she is here for me then I'll make sure I put on a good show. The thing that I can't do is allow it to get to me. I have worked to damn hard for it fall apart now!"

Cyn arced a brow as she saw the nerves smiled as she for once saw Melanie uneasy which was a rarity. Melanie always had her shit together never seemed to have an off day so she replied

"Ditto."

Melanie used that knowledge to keep her head in the game. She watched as Cyn cut to the basket Melanie threw the ball up in an alley pass Cyn capitalized and the crowd erupted including the blonde. Melanie sent a smile and a wink her way. She couldn't help it dammit the hottest chick in the stadium was here for her. She had to show off a little bit she wanted her to suffer just as she was and she knew she was she could tell out in the parking lot. Brandy felt her heart flip as she watched the brunette look her way and wink. Damn the woman packed a punch she had to have a sample. She felt herself throb, she ran a shaky hand through her hair. Shelly was toast had to be toast this woman was hers had to be hers

By the end of the game Melanie had 36 points 9 assists 3 steals she wiped her face with a towel. She watched as the blonde walked her way. She shook her head wondering why her body decided to tremble now. Melanie brushed it off as she cleared her throat and lock eyes with the drop dead gorgeous woman. Yeah she wanted her she truly did but the thing was she didn't want to look like a fool when she told her she wasn't available and it turn out to just be business so she would play it tough had too.

"What do you want?"

Brandy had to remind herself to stay professional even though she was full of want and all she wanted to do was pull her close and sample those lips. She knew she had to get business out of the way first had to for pap so she cocked her hip as she looked into those deep blue pools.

"May we talk? I'll be waiting by my car."

Melanie watched as the blonde walked toward the door. Melanie sputtered and went to the locker room the way she was just so cocky had Melanie flustered. How did she know she was going to show? Hell she didn't even know if she was or not she found the coach waiting which caught her by surprise she cleared her throat trying to hide the fit she just had. She felt her face turn red and heat up,

"Red Hot?"

"Yes coach?"

Brenda smiled as she heard the nerves in the young woman's voice,

"Good game!"

Melanie nodded she had to admit it was a test and it wasn't the game itself that was the test the test laid squarely on the shoulders of a blonde who had just barged into her life. Tore it all apart. Melanie breathed a sigh of relief for she thought it would be about that very blonde and quite frankly she didn't think she could handle a conversation like that right now,

"Thanks coach."

Brenda watched as Mels sat on the bench Brenda folded her arms and spoke

"Loved the way you handled Sal"

"Yeah I know."

Melanie ran a hand through her hair as she spoke,

"Totally different from the last time you played against her."

They both agreed last time Melanie was totally man handled she fixed her issues so they could bring home the cup even though she knew that the way she played was because she needed to focus and what drove her was a set of brown eyes and a 38 bust.

"Yeah I just had to get my mind clear."

"Made me proud!"

Melanie looked into her eyes Brenda knew she needed to hear that

Melanie sat on the bench. She closed her eyes trying to clear her head but all she could see was the blonde with big breasts and a piercing set of brown eyes. She grabbed her bag and headed to her car. When she found the blond leaning against the Audi she felt her body betray her. Melanie headed to the civic she needed to gather herself before she handled anything with this heart throb. Brandy smiled and spoke

"Finally!"

Melanie closed her eyes, sure she wanted to do nothing but sit in front of this woman and enjoy her company but she just was not up for the task. She needed to let loose and just breathe so she spoke,

"Coach held me up. Look I don't know you. I don't even know why you are wanting to talk to me but I am going to tell you I can't talk to you tonight. I'm going out with my friends and celebrating, find me tomorrow!"

"No you don't know me but I know you and Melanie Brooks like it or not you will get to know me and who knows you just might like what you find."

"Look lady I only met you today and you already clog my thoughts I just can't handle anymore right now."

Brandy smiled as she moved a step closer. She couldn't help herself she needed to see the fire in her eyes one more time.

"I clog your thoughts huh well Ms. Brooks you make me hot so hot. I haven't had that and let me tell you I am trying so hard right now not to take that mouth and find that taste."

Brandy took Melanie's mouth she couldn't help it she needed a sample at that moment she couldn't think like the scout she was right at that moment she was thinking like the woman she was and when she finally had those lips and their tongues danced she thought she heard a moan damn she felt herself grow wet Melanie was met with more want she was totally enveloped with passion she found herself totally engulfed she never knew anything could feel this good brandy knew she had to pull away knew if she didn't that she stood to not have a chance so she pulled away she found Melanie still reeling with want brandy smiled

"You ok?"

Melanie cleared her throat as she spoke

"You better not have a girlfriend blondie, you kiss me before I know your name. Hell you kiss me before

I know you period and here I stand wanting you so damn bad."

"My name is Brandy, Brandy Hawke. I would tell you why I'm here but when I do get you naked I want you to know that I want you naked I don't mix business and pleasure honey."

"So are you available?"

"As a matter of fact I am."

Melanie ran a hand through her hair.

"This is crazy I never do anything like this this is crazy I got to go"

"Wait when can I talk to you?"

"I will find you tomorrow sometime I just got to get my head around all of this."

"You do that but just know that when I sleep tonight. I'm thinking of you"

"See you say things like that and it makes me vibrate!"

Brandy smiled as she looked into her eyes. Melanie let her pull her close.

"I mean it Melanie this isn't a gimmick I do want you."

"You don't know me?"

"I know how you make me feel."

"You just met me today. How can you possibly know you want me?"

"Trust me, I know I see it in your eyes you want me too."

THE PARTY CONTINUES

"I gotta go."

"Fine I'll let you go for now baby but know I'm here for business and pleasure and you have a date with me on both."

Melanie couldn't help but smile she didn't want to think she just wanted to feel she found Brandy's mouth this time she lead the charge this time she was the one feed the fire this time totally catching brandy off guard she felt a hunger like no other she was captivated she was the one who cried out into Melanie's mouth Melanie pulled away she held a smile

"You ok blondie?"

"I will be so I will catch you tomorrow."

She watched the blond nod and turn she headed to her car Melanie never in her life did she think she would ever be making out in the parking lot after a game and especially with a drop dead gorgeous woman boy she sure needed a drink. She climbed in and set out to Cyn's house. the pub was their way of celebrating after winning the championship and now it sounded so inviting because she needed to settle her nerves she pulled in and she found Cyn and Sara wrestling she climbed out chuckling

"What happened this time?"

"She stole my keys!"

"Did she now?"

Cyn looked in Melanie's eyes she saw humor and Melanie's face,

"Oh shut it PG!"

Melanie folded her hands waited a few minutes she didn't have time for this she wanted to get a drink on needed too so she spoke

"I was looking to head to the pub but since you all have other plans I think I'll turn in"

Melanie headed to her car she heard Cynthia tell Sarah to stop

"Okay okay we're going to!"

Melanie turned around with a smile accepted the hugs and ignored the looks they gave each other

"I have to get dressed I'm not going like this."

She knew if she was going to the pub there would be a chance of her meeting the blonde and she wanted to dress to impress

"Right right you left a bag at my place"

"Good looks like I'll be needing it."

"Maybe you'll see the blonde there?"

Melanie remembered the kiss she felt the want she didn't want them to catch on she couldn't deal with that right now so she said

"Oh maybe I don't care if I do?"

"I saw the looks i saw the way you all went at each other mels you can't lie to me it's written all over your face."

Melanie rolled her eyes as she followed Cynthia in her apartment to get dressed for the pub. Brandy Hawke was in the Bluegrass State cursed herself for forgetting her thermals since it was winter in Kentucky that's what she gets thinking it was sunny and 75 everywhere with a shrug she went into the musky bar it was rather small she had to nod in approval at the relics on the walls the bar was small the crowd was unimaginably large she worked her way to the bar

"What'll it be Miss?"

She looked at the aging bartender why did it seem fitting to be in a bar when all she really wanted to do was take the brunette who stole her heart with one glance back to her hotel and really get to know her she shivered with anticipation

"Jack on the rocks"

He nodded as he began to make her drink then ask

> "Coming right up, say haven't seen the likes of you around here must be new?"

> "You can say that"

> "What brings you to our neck of the woods?"

That question could be answered in various ways but she kept it to business

> "Well a little business."

About that time a group of people erupted into cheers. Brandy watched the bartenders smile grow and followed his line of vision her eyes landed on the very brunette. She needed to talk too she felt her oxygen level plummet as she watched her come in with several other girls oddly she felt a hint of jealousy rise when she watched them hug the one woman she wanted more than anything

> "I was wondering if she'd make it?"

Brandy watched the brunette walk to the crowd at the back table she wore a suit it was black with pink Pinstripes her Fedora was black she were Converses with a suit Brandy had to chuckle she already knew she was a goner she took a sip of her jack and turned back to the bartender

> "That's Melanie's overdue celebration if you ask me she worked her tail off to get to where she is today she deserves it."

That caught Brandy's attentions so she asked,

> "What do you mean overdue?"

> "See well all she ever does is work, work, work. She never makes time for herself."

Brandy sipped on her Jack she hated how her grandfather sent her on Wild Goose chases this time he sent her to land the infamous red hot from the Wildcats what he failed to tell her was she was coming to Kentucky to lose her heart to a basketball phenomenon who kissed like hell. Brandy closed her eyes she couldn't get the kiss out of her mind. The way Melanie had her all tied up in knots was totally a whole new ball game for her. She knew Melanie would be a great ball player hell the numbers spoke volumes what she never counted on was falling for the very person she was coming here to sign and she didn't even know where it would lead. All she knew was how she felt she finished her drink and decided to get out before she lost it and had Melanie under her she knew that would take time.

"Leaving us so soon?"

She locked eyes with the bartender she didn't want too but knew it was best for all that were involved.

"Yeah."

"Have another one you look like you could use it? Besides the guy in the seat behind you bought you one."

Brandy closed her eyes fuck she hated it when men bought her drinks that usually meant that they wanted her for one thing she wasn't going to pass up a drink that was for sure besides she could watch Melanie that was worth the fight she was going to have to do later

"Can't pass up a free drink."

Brandy set back down was about to take a drink when she felt the bump in her back and the jack on her hands.

"Oh shit! Cynthia- sorry man!"

Brandy turn face-to-face with the very Burnett she had been watching all night. The very reason she was here freezing her nubbins off the one woman who stole her heart from hello Brandy, locked eyes on those lips Melanie saw the fire in Brandy's eyes cause all was good till jack hit the table. Melanie felt her body turn hot. She saw the kiss replaying in her mind she had to admit Brandy was sexy pissed. Melanie hid the smirk and spoke,

"Look it was an accident."

Brandy shot Cynthia a stern look she shut up Cyn wasn't tangling with the blonde totally. Melanie's job she could she the connection. She secretly cheered she knew the both of them were on the same page they just needed a nudge in the right direction. Press or not Melanie wanted the blonde and Cyn knew that she just was shy when it came to putting herself out there so if Cyn had to spill jack on the blonde to make it happen so be it Cyn chuckled

"Hell chick, I'll buy you another one!"

Brandy locked eyes with Melanie she wanted to have her attention on her so she would have her buy her one but with a exception.

"Fair enough if you drink one drink with me?"

Melanie's blue pools landed on Brandy's dark ones she knew the blonde was here for her. She knew the fire between them was real and she also knew that the blonde was in fits but she wasn't going to make it easy. Melanie had to admit she was hot and that she packed a punch that hit her so hard she thought she had slammed into a brick wall. The kiss held power she gave the blonde a once over she had on slacks and blouse definitely not a booster but she didn't look like a recruit either. Melanie surprised herself when she heard an okay come from her lips.

"But-"

Melanie turn to Cynthia and shewed her off one way to deal with the Enemy was to keep them close she chuckled when she heard Cynthia mutter and Retreat to the table in the back corner Melanie sat down by Brandy Melanie spoke

"So blondie I can tell your new here what brings you to the pub?"

"Oh down time what brings you here?"

"Celebration."

"So I heard, you care to elaborate?"

"My Team just won the championship me being the MVP felt fitting besides you should know you were there!"

Brandy locked eyes with Melanie at that moment Brandy could have sworn time stood still

"Yeah I watched the game. Congrats you played a really good game, definitely worth it"

Melanie put her drink down she cleared her throat

"Ok brandy all jokes aside why were you at my game?"

"I told you I don't mix business with pleasure"

Brandy said as she took a sip of her drink trying to hide her nerves Melanie picked up her drink took a sip then she spoke

"I don't understand you seriously you kiss like hell I mean hell tore me up but you will not tell me why you are here"

Melanie watched as brandy grew kind of uncomfortable then she watched as she put her hands on the table Melanie found herself lost in thought about just what those hands could be doing she cleared her throat as brandy spoke

"It's not that I won't Melanie it's that I want the two separated"

Brandy arced a brow as Melanie countered

"Why"

She cleared her throat as she answered simply by this time she needed another drink being in close proximity of the woman in itself was a buzz

"Because you're the business that brought me here"

Melanie couldn't help but get uncomfortable she didn't know what to expect and she knew the last thing she wanted to do was make an ass of herself in front of the one woman she wanted to ask to the award ceremony so she cleared her throat and stated

"Well I'm tired"

Melanie locked eyes with brandy they neither one had to say a word they knew both were in for a long while brandy answered

"Night"

Brandy watch her get up and walk out the door the bartender stared at Brandy. Brandy spoke,

"What?"

"You Got It Bad"

Brandy turned to face the bartender she was tired of denying it and couldn't do anything until she found the right moment to actually tell her who she was so she admitted it

"Yes I do"

She watched as his smile grew and his eyes light up

"Well hell finally!"

That statement caught her off guard so she asked

"Finally what?"

She watched as he grew serious she could tell there was a story about Melanie that she didn't know one she didn't want to know until Melanie was ready to tell her about it

"She has a shot of getting out of here"

"Maybe she did leave"

Brandy loved the idea of Melanie leaving with her ooh how great would it be to have Melanie right beside her no formalities just them together no barriers she smiled as he said

"She'll be back"

Brandy stood up paid for drinks and headed to the door when a guy caught her arm

"Hey"

Brandy found the middle aged man standing behind her he wore a crew cut big biceps brandy smirked and turned walked out the door the guy followed her she knew she would have to fight and the damn sad thing about it Melanie was still there she cursed as he shouted

"I know what I can do with you"

She rolled her eyes as she turned to face him and countered

"Yeah and I know what I can do with you so be a good dog and go inside"

She watched his face turn red she could have sworn she saw steam coming from his ears by this time there was a crowd she was sure by this time Melanie was somewhere in the crowd she didn't want to have to show Melanie this side

"David quit!"

Brandy recognize the voice as the bartender she watch the highly intoxicated man sputter she was hoping that the man would listen and she didn't have to fight but it hardly ever worked that way

"Not yet this bitch is going to get it!"

THE PARTY CONTINUES

Brandy wanted this over with she wanted out of there and to just go to the hotel and rest already

"Anytime"

Melanie stood in the back she saw the guy she couldn't help but be scared Cynthia beside her Cynthia spoke

"David will eat her up!"

But it was when she watched the fire reach those eyes she knew the blonde knew what she was doing so she had to side with brandy

"I doubt it I have a feeling that sexy piece of flesh packs power"

"Don't tell me your goo goo over that bimbo"

"Shut it or I will mention Stacy"

"Ouch fine!"

Melanie bit her lip in anticipation as she watched Brandi set David tried to grab her found himself on the ground Brandy's foot on his throat

"I told you to go inside you refuse now I'm telling you to leave me and any other female alone!"

Brandy watched as he tried to move

"Damn bitch!"

"I'm going to let you up. Your best bet will be to retreat."

"Not on your life!"

"It's your face."

Brandy let him up sure enough he came at her again she knocked him out cold the crowd got silent Brandy's eyes landed on Melanie's.

Melanie could see the sadness before she picked her purse up and headed to her car. Melanie felt her body heat up as she watched the car drive off.

"Oh hell Melanie done fell in love."

Melanie spoke more to herself than to anyone else.

"She's definitely got a punch."

"Just don't piss her off!"

"Got to see her again for that."

Everyone was whispering about what had happened with David. Melanie couldn't help but think about it herself. Although her mind was working a little different like those biceps, that face, and the strength. She came to when Cynthia's spoke,

"Are we heading home yet?"

"Oh yeah."

Melanie grabbed her keys they headed to her car she heard that voice the voice that seemed to stop her heart she closed her eyes as she spoke her heart fluttered she had done thought she was gone.

"What?"

Brandy walked to her she needed to explain what had happened.

"We need to talk"

Melanie tossed her wallet in the car and turned to face Brandy,

"What about?"

Brandy ran a hand over her brow took a deep breath trying to hide the frustration.

"We just do."

Brandy saw the tired look on Melanie's face.

THE PARTY CONTINUES

"Look I've had a long night I'm beat."

"Why don't we grab a bite to eat?"

She took Melanie's hand and put it too her lips.

"I don't even know you. Highly doubt that would happen. All I know is that you kiss like hell and can handle yourself pretty damn good."

Brandy said fuck it so she laid it out plain.

"Fine I'm here on behalf of the Flames gm to see if we can negotiate a deal to have you playing for the Flames next season."

Brandy had the satisfaction of seeing the shock on Melanie's face. Brandy watched the brunettes face process the information. Melanie clears her throat,

"You said flames?"

"Don't think I stuttered, it seems I finally have your attention."

Brandy held her hands in front of her the brunette stood all of 5'8" foot her brown hair was a shag. Brandy cleared her throat as she found herself wanting to brush the loose locks out of her eyes so she put her hands in her pockets.

"The Flames want me?"

"Have had an eye on you since high school."

Brandy could see the wheels rolling in her mind she smiled,

"High School?"

Melanie couldn't think all of this information hit her so fast she found it was even harder to breathe. She couldn't believe that this was real could she be dreaming?

Brandy answered,

> "Yeah I didn't want to let you know like this but I realized it was the only way to get your attention. I am usually a little more graceful with my approach."

Melanie dropped her bag let the tears fall. She couldn't hide her emotion finally all her hard work was paying off. She looked at the blonde who just stood there she expected something like the blonde to mock her or laugh at her but she just stood there Melanie stood up and grabbed her bag. She just stood there with that earnest look she looked at the blonde again,

> "Sorry it's just this has been my ultimate goal in life. Just hard to process all of this at once!"

> "No don't be let it process because I want to know you'll be there May 1st!"

> "I'll be there. I work too hard not to be."

Brandy noted that she let her hand touch Melanie on the shoulder.

> "Good you okay?"

> "Yeah I'll be okay!"

> "You sure?"

> "Yep."

Melanie climbed in her car before Brandy could ask any more questions and headed out of the parking lot. Brandy sighed and headed to her own car. Damn she shook her head every time as she prepared to call George to give her the address she needed the documents filled out or nothing was going to be going through as she opened the door she heard someone call for her. She saw a coach coming her way.

> "Hey"

"So?"

"So we want her I told her. She said yes but I didn't get all I needed to make sure we have her."

"Honey it's been her dream. Here is her address make sure that kid gets out of here."

"Yes ma'am!"

"Nice meeting you."

Brandy's cop sense was itching damn she had more personal questions than she did professional questions. She looked at the address she smiled as she set the address into her GPS set out to see Melanie one more time her phone rang.

"Hello?"

"Oh and Miss Hawke, we have a banquet Thursday night. Why don't you come?"

"Okay?"

"See you there, bye."

Brandy wiped her brow as she pulled into the apartment complex next to the college she saw Melanie still in her car. Brandy pulled up beside of the only woman who stole her oxygen with just a glance. At that moment, she locked eyes with Brandy's blue ones she felt her heart skip a beat. She found herself heating up as their eyes locked Brandy didn't want to look out of sorts so she cleared her throat as she grabbed the file that needed filled out that was the whole reason Brandy was there. Well that's what she told herself anyway George wanted red hot committed to the flames then that's exactly what he'd get. Brandy climbed out as did Melanie she took one step toward Brandy, closed her door.

"Yeah?"

Brandy smiled as she looked into Melanie's eyes.

"Melanie there is paperwork with this, we want you, and you said you wanted this then let's make it official."

"Official?"

"Yeah"

Brandy held up the folder indicating she was serious.

"See I can tell you all day but at the end of the day it's the bottom line your signature that speaks. That actually makes it official that tells the GM that you really want to be there."

Melanie grabs her bags. Brandy sighed as she figured she'd have to play chase again she rubbed her brow.

"Come on! I'm still not sure about this"

Brandy followed Melanie into the complex to the elevators closed her eyes as she spoke. Melanie could see the woman looked like she was about ready to fall over her eyes were half-closed then she heard her speak.

"You sure you're okay?"

"Yeah just a lot to take in in a short notice. I mean I spent my whole life dreaming about this day and all I can do is try to breathe. When I was a kid I figured I'd be jumping up and down but what I feel right now I'm full of terror, what if I'm not good enough, what if I mess up it's just really scary."

"I know but from what I seen at the game tonight that's how you feel right at home on the court. I mean as you said yourself you have worked so hard. I don't think you're going to forget it on the blink of a dime!"

THE PARTY CONTINUES

Brandy got off the elevator as a phone ring she locked eyes with Melanie. She had been dreading this call she knew George would call and see if she had the famous Red Hot. Little did he know she was doing all she could to just sit down and talk with her hearing the phone ring again she figured she better take it.

"Hey Gramps!"

"Well, do we have her?"

"Not exactly yet?"

"What's the holdup?"

"Why don't you ask her?"

Brandy handed the phone to Melanie figured she let her deal with a headache for a while she locked eyes with Melanie she saw the question look in her eyes.

"It's for you."

Brandy handed the phone over wishing she had a jack on rocks right now. Yeah that's what she needed a stiff drink and a soft bed.

"Me? Hello?"

"So Red Hot what does it take for you to be on this team? What can I offer you to ensure that I have a starting point guard?"

"I don't understand. Why are you so eager to get me?"

"Look Red Hot I know you know you're the top point guard in the country and look kid I want you on this team if it's money I can have Brandy write you a check right now the check would be in your hand."

"It's not the money."

"Hold it honey, never start like that, what do you want?"

"I want to play ball, be somebody, make a name for myself. I don't want to go into this with the high hopes that I will be a starter and ended up on the bench for say 4 years I want to sign with a team going in knowing that I'm going to be able to make my statement!"

"See how hard was that. Listen deary I can assure you that you are going to be a starter on this team. I want a ring. I want a championship and you're going to get that for me but not by being on the bench. Brandy will handle the details look forward to meeting you soon."

Melanie handed the phone to Brandy who put it to her ear. She was hoping that her grandfather had hung up but she heard that voice.

"Cut her check!"

"What?"

"Yeah you know signing bonus. I don't want to lose her and with her having doubts. I'm going to lose a few grand too gain my winning point guard who knows she might bring a few of her teammates along."

"You sneaky clever old man you. That's what you're hoping for so Cynthia and maybe Sarah will come along as well this ain't just about Melanie you're wanting to get your whole team from this team you clever old man!"

"Well I wouldn't have the best record around if I wasn't clever chickadee but seriously she's the best Brandy treat her that way!"

"If you say so Gramps if you say so!"

"Thanks honey by the way you sound like hell."

"I wonder why I get off of a stint to come down here and play tag along."

"Just do what I told you see you soon!"

"Bye Gramps!"

Brandy followed Melanie into her apartment where she was immediately met with a growl. She immediately identified the source as a beautiful tan german shepherd she heard Melanie bark out.

"Duke, friend go lay down!"

Brandy watched as the beautiful dog lay where he stood. Melanie locked her door dropped her bag on the couch and went down the hall. Brandy went to the kitchen table. Melanie came back out then went out the back down the hall to the elevator and down to the ball court, Brandy followed.

"You know at some point we do have to deal with this paperwork I do have a life to get back to."

"Fine we'll talk but after I do my reps."

"Fine I'll wait!"

Melanie shot her a look how was she to concentrate with a drop dead gorgeous woman standing under the basket. She knew the best way for her to concentrate was just to get the whole ordeal over and done with so she put the ball on the rack and went to Brandy.

"Fine let's get this over with."

"What about your reps?"

"Honey with you around I'd miss everything."

Brandy shot her look and let that smile bloom.

"I think you do fine you're used to huge crowds."

"Yeah well none of them hold a 36 bust and piercing blue eyes!"

Brandy busted out laughing that sound had Melanie falling even harder. She climbed in the elevator. Brandy sat on the leather sectional and explained every form to Melanie it took an hour but when the last paper was signed both ladies let out a relieving breath. Brandy stood gathered her papers started putting them in the manila folder she turned to go then remembered Gramps request pulled out the check she handed it to Melanie.

"Oh this is a sign on bonus. Gramps wanted me to give it to you if you committed!"

"You're kidding right?"

"No actually I'm not and 3.9 minutes he's going to call and ask if you sat down and filled out the paperwork and if you are okay with the terms and if you're okay with the amount that's on the check?"

Melanie looked at the numbers she then looked at Brandy even with her part time job in the last 3 years. She knew wouldn't add up to the amount on the check she shot Brandy a cynical look.

"Is this a trick? Do you think I'm an idiot?"

"No it's not a trick. No I don't think you're an idiot. What's with you being cynical?"

"Call it experience."

"Well start trusting people."

Melanie put the check in her billfold then Melanie turned to the blonde with a confident look.

"Give me your number!"

"What?"

"I need your number in case this check bounces sky high."

"It won't."

"Still hand it over."

Brandy blew out an exasperated breath and wrote it on the paper on the table. Just as she got done right on cue her phone buzzed to life.

"Oh speak of the cheetah!"

Brandy winked as she answered the phone.

Melanie found herself in uncharted waters. She found she wanted the blonde usually women came to her. Sure she'd have fun. Enjoy the company and leave but with this particular blonde things seem different she felt things wouldn't be so easy she was brought to by the very blonde talking.

"What?"

"He wants to talk to you."

"Oh okay."

"Hey Lassie how's the number?"

"Big!"

"Just bring me rings and get us some winning records!"

"I will sir."

"Oh, call me Gramps, Lassie"

"Gramps!"

"Yes see you soon!"

"Soon?"

"Yeah conditioning starts March for the rookies!"

"Okay see you soon!"

March she only had a few months before she had the rest of her life starting. Talking about wind sinking in her lungs she locked eyes with Brandy who could see the wheels rolling. March that's just a few months away. Brandy still didn't grab the folder. Melanie didn't want her to leave she was fighting herself.

"Got time for a drink?"

"Always have time for a drink!"

Melanie smiled as she grabbed her wallet. Brandy felt her heart flip as Melanie grabbed her shades.

"You can drive!"

"As you wish Mel's!"

Melanie closed her eyes just hearing her name come off those lips was a mini orgy.

"Same place as last night?"

"I only go to the pub!"

"Works for me."

In the pub Brandy found herself in the corner. Melanie sipping on her coors. Brandy sipped on hers, jack on the rocks, Melanie looked into those piercing blues and spoke,

"I'm a straight forward gal and even though I chance getting knocked down I must ask. Are you available?"

Brandy looked in her eyes and smiled that half-smile glad she'd called it off with Shelly.

"Yes Mel's I'm available!"

"Seriously?"

"Yes I'm Free. Why?"

Melanie felt her throat slam shut. Brandy arched a brow. Which had Melanie wanting to moan. Melanie finally spoke,

"Because I find you sexy and be stupid not to ask."

"Well now, thank you little lady but I must say the feeling is mutual, are you available?"

"Yes Hawke if I weren't we wouldn't be having this conversation!"

"No there's something you need to know. I'm a detective I go under on occasion my job is growling. I spend more time working than I do anything."

Melanie ran a hand on her cheek and let it go lower she leaned in and spoke,

"Good to know now my turn. I understand your job I know just what the job entails I myself am a criminal justice major. I graduate next week the job is not an issue with me."

Brandy felt her body vibrate. Melanie smiled as she let her hand go up Brandy's thigh. Melanie watched as the blonde closed her eyes. Brandy felt her system come to life like never before she whispered,

"When do you leave?"

"Gramps wants the papers finalized as soon as possible."

"Let me have you something we both need."

"Need?"

"Yeah since I'm not going to see you for a minute."

"Are you wanting to be my girlfriend Red Hot?"

Melanie saw the smile she knew that Brandy was joking. She let her hand run up Brandy's thigh

"Baby I want to be your only."

"If I date you, you will be!"

"If?"

Brandy chuckled then she stood threw a few bills on the table then she pulled Melanie to her.

"Yeah I still need to see about tonight."

Melanie beamed with pride as she locked eyes with Brandy.

"Baby I'm going to rock your world."

"Really?"

"Two things. I'm sure of on this earth that's basketball and my talent in bed."

Brandy stepped aside and let Melanie through.

"Lead the way princess!"

"I plan on leading you to my bed."

Brandy couldn't park the car soon enough. She was so hungry. She couldn't get enough of Melanie. As they entered the complex, Melanie had her against the wall, as they entered Melanie's apartment Brandy begged for Melanie to begin.

"Easy baby with you. I'm taking my time."

Melanie eased Brandy's back against the wall. She ran her hand over the very erect nipples this action alone left Brandy putty. She captured her mouth taking the hunger deeper making both fight clothing and crave more. Melanie ran her hands over Brandy's breast!

"Fuck, pure beauty, love that tat!"

THE PARTY CONTINUES

"Turn off the most!"

"Hell no, turns me on!"

Melanie found herself on top of Brandy. She wanted to take in the sexy picture. She never thought someone of Brandy's caliber would want her. So she was taking in the moment and if it was only this moment. She had what she wanted. To make sure it was an unforgettable moment for both. She ran her knee over the hotspot she smiled as she undid Brandy's pants. She didn't expect anything less she smiled as she ran a hand over the small patch of hair. Oh so nice and tidy. Melanie let her tongue explore sending Brandy arching back. Melanie loved this the most. She took not this time she enjoyed the sounds that Brandy made odd. She found that her enjoyment wasn't with a quick roll. This was different. Brandy cried out as Melanie begin the charge. Brandy couldn't think didn't want to right now. She wanted to feel she felt the edge inching closer. Melanie found her mouth as she slide her finger on the g spot. That's all it took they race together, hot and sweaty, as they cried out in unison. Melanie stood shocked as Brandy held her so close. She never had that. Melanie held her close all night.

Brandy smiled when she awakened to find Melanie still holding her. Brandy found her mouth and was well on her way when Melanie awoken orgasm.

"Hawke, be careful I might just fall in love with you!"

"Oh yeah. Same goes for you!"

Melanie kissed her. Damn this time Brandy knew she gave her everything. Brandy got dressed. Melanie watched as she put her blouses on!

"When I first saw you, you brought a part of me to life, a part I thought I lost years ago. When you bumped into me I knew I needed a few minutes with you!"

"I'd say you got more!"

Brandy looked at the brunette with a shag. She was built, still held a petite body, Brandy wanted to soak in every detail. She watched as Melanie slid on the shorts and a t-shirt that simple gesture was sexy as hell. She muttered to herself. Melanie smiled,

"You okay?"

Brandy found her mouth she wasn't gentle. She was hungry. She feasted just as quickly as she feasted she pulled away.

"You're in my system, Brooks. I'm not sure how I feel about that."

"You're in mine too, Hawke. Like you it's new to me."

Brandy let herself into the hotel room. She slung her bag on the bed. She herself landed on the bed sent out the victory text and fell asleep.

Brandy awoke to her phone ringing. She cursed but answered,

"Hey!"

Melanie felt chills of excitement as she smiled,

"So I see the number works."

"Of course it does."

"I woke you, didn't I?"

"No I'm right as rain."

"Good let me in."

"What?"

"Open up silly!"

Brandy opened her door to a very energetic Melanie who walked up to Brandy and kissed her squarely on the mouth then went and laid the food on the table. Melanie saw the disgruntled look kind of like the way she looked last night that gave Melanie a very hot feeling with Brandy standing there with her disheveled hair. She was so sexy!

"So?"

"I thought I'd bring you breakfast and ask if you had plans today."

"No I don't have plans today other than sleep."

"Good I want to show you around."

"Oh okay you always this energetic in the mornings?"

"No but thanks to awesome sex I am this morning if it helps I brought coffee."

"That helps."

Brandy took the coffee closed her eyes thanking God for coffee. Melanie noticed the scar on her upper arm and she loved the tat. She oddly found she wanted to see that tan body again. Brandy stood up,

"Let me shower real quick."

"Sure no hurry!"

Brandy grabbed her bag and went in the bathroom 20 minutes later. She came out in a blouse and jeans. Her hair was up in a tail, earrings showing although Melanie couldn't get her eyes off of that hot pink bra. She felt apart of her come to life a part of her that she never knew she had. She bit her lip as she let her eyes linger on the very blonde who kept her up last night.

"Ready?"

"Definitely!"

Melanie went to the door sighed as she lead Brandy to her honda civic. Brandy climbed in and Melanie set the car in motion. Melanie didn't really have a plan but she wanted Brandy to enjoy herself for the day. She so wanted to spend every minute she had with Brandy. Brandy leaned her head back as she stole a glance at the brunette.

> "I have never been to Kentucky until now."

> "Never?"

Melanie licked her lips as she guided the honda out of the city.

> "Nope kind of nice to see the Bluegrass State. When I found out I was coming I was kind of shocked!"

Brandy locked eyes with Melanie then she smiled

> "I'm glad I came."

> "Well I hope you enjoy the ride. I'm going to visit my old coach in Lewis County quite a ride but well I hope you enjoy the ride."

Brandy knew she would enjoy the ride as long as she was spending time with Melanie. Brandy looked at her she was smiling totally different from the girl last night filled with sexual tension so intense the thought alone had Brandy aching for more. Which made Brandy so want to know her more.

> "So since we're stuck in this car. How about a game of 20 questions?"

> "Sure I go first."

> "How old are you?"

> "27 and you?"

> "23."

Melanie smiled as she bit her lip. She never felt someone send her system into overdrive like Brandy did. She loved the view. She spoke,

THE PARTY CONTINUES

"So you said something last night about how you loved your job?"

"I'm a detective for the LAPD."

Brandy watched as Melanie's eyes grew large then show a puzzled look.

"So what, you're a detective by day Scout by night?"

"No, George Hawke is my grandfather. I'll simply help him from time to time"

"Oh okay."

"When did you decide you wanted to go into law enforcement?"

"You can say it's a family business, how about you when did you decide it was ball?"

"You can say since I was old enough to understand the game."

"Do you like roses?"

"Yeah oddly. Do I find tulips are my favorite? Red and white ones and do you like roses?"

"I'm not much into flowers so you can say I'm a sucker for a bouquet of red roses on Valentine's Day."

Melanie kept that as a mental note then she spoke.

"Favorite movie?"

"Any romance is okay. I'm a sucker for a good horror film as well. What about you? What's your favorite movie?"

"Well to be honest horror films scare the crap out of me so I'm a big chick flick kind of gal."

"Ideal date night?"

Melanie was silent for a minute like she was lost in thought. Brandy stole a glance,

"Call me crazy but a favorite date for me would be for my date to cook me a meal and then with our shoes off. We sip wine under the stars just something very romantic to me so how about Miss Brandy what's her dream date?"

"Mine is taking the one I date to a small but nice restaurant not too flashy but just to show her that she deserves the best and my attention. Then come home and sip wine shoes off under the stars."

"First kiss?"

"Brittany Tolman, 9th grade at a swim party how about Miss Hawke? Who was the first lucky girl?"

"Grace short 12th grade high school prom."

"Really I figured you would have like a whole black book or something."

"Believe it or not I didn't look like this and in high school. Plus everyone wanted me because my grandpa had to be very selective."

Brandy spoke this time. She was more quiet her finger ran lightly up Melanie's arm. They locked eyes for a brief second then she spoke very very quietly

"First time?"

"Nothing."

"What?"

"Brandy Hawke, 23, at my pad."

"Why didn't you tell me? I would have made it special."

"You did it was special."

Somehow Brandy felt like she let her down. Melanie spoke up,

"That's just a rough topic for me to discuss. I'm happy with the way things happened and I wouldn't change anything anyway, how about you?"

"Grace, short, 18, 12th grade prom."

Brandy cleared her throat knowing something had happened and then asked,

"Would you date me if you knew nothing about the flames and Gramps?"

"Honey, you took my breath away when I saw you the first time. I could care less about who's related to whom. How about you? Would you date me knowing that I've been through things that way?"

"Same for you Mels. I found myself wanting to get to know you more."

Melanie sighed in relief as she drove up the mountain Brandy love the view of the trees. Something about the trees the winding roads and the deep valley views just captivated her. She never seen anything like that. Where she came from? She cleared her throat and spoke,

"So Melanie dream home?"

"I've always dreamed of owning a pad by the ocean so that when I wake up I can see the sunrise over the ocean with a pool. Maybe a hot tub. How about you? What is your type of dream home?"

"Well I don't know about dream home but I've always wanted a cabin in the woods somewhere that way maybe I and the person I love could vacation there. Maybe around Christmas or something because I've never seen snow before."

Melanie caught her eye and asked

"You've never seen snow before?"

"No darling. I live in California remember we don't get snow."

"Be cold but well worth it. A white Christmas is magical definitely need to experience that,"

Brandy saw the small house the yard was covered with leaves the wood stacked up by the door smoke coming from the chimney. Melanie looked into Brandy's eyes.

"Thank you for coming up here with me truly means a lot."

"You kidding. I'm having fun."

Melanie tapped her shoulder playfully

"Yeah right."

"Seriously Melanie I'm having a blast!"

Melanie climbed out as Brandy did. Melanie came to her and took her hand,

"I'm so excited!"

About that time the door opened and Brandy saw the old man come out.

"Well hell its Mel's. Fran get out here!"

"Well I'll be come here sugar give me some loves."

Brandy oddly felt right at home. The conversation was lite and the laughs plenty. She saw Melanie so happy she loved her smile it was so contagious as was her laughter.

> "So Mel's what brought you all the way out here from Lexington. We know you won the championship should be out there celebrating your success!"

> "Yeah played against Richter and Sal."

> "You had her kiddo you wasn't letting her inside your head you owned it just like I knew you would. Just like I told you you made me proud of you kiddo. Wouldn't have done any different myself."

Melanie blushed she knew she never heard her old coach talk like that. She knew he meant it he was the reason she found basketball the reason she had dreams the reason she knew she would do the flames good. She owed everything to him and Francine she stood knew that if she displayed her feelings to them in front of Brandy that she would embarrass them.

> "Thank you, sir! That means a lot."

Melanie cleared her throat shot a glance in Brandy's direction.

> "I'm actually here because I'm going to L.A. after this semester."

> "What?"

She saw the confusion in both of her parents faces. She smiled as she ran a hand across her brow she hurried before Francine began one of her lectures on responsibility and choices in life.

> "Yeah seems that the flames love me so much that they want me there ASAP! Seems that you weren't the only ones blew away by yesterday's game."

She heard Francine muffle her excitement and Paul stood with that beaming smile and embraced her in a big hug.

> "Well kiddo you did. It not that I didn't think that you would. I knew that you would I just am so damn proud of you!"

> "I know this is my dream. I have dreamt of that flames jersey ever since I played for the lions when I was notified I flipped out thinking it was a joke when it hit me that they were serious I about melted."

Brandy cleared her throat and spoke

> "The Flames are so lucky to have Ms. Harper. Just know that while she is in L.A that we will do our best to make sure she is taken care of."

> "Y-Your the recruiter?"

> "Among other things, sir!"

> "Melanie isn't a bench warmer!"

Brandy kindly held up a hand smiled shot a glance to Melanie she stood in her cop stance.

> "Trust me George fully plans on utilizing Red Hot. He wants a ring and knows that the only way to get it is playing the very player that made the top 300 with as complex of a game that Melanie brings to the game. There is not a single GM in the game that wouldn't play her first string. I'm just glad that she signed with us."

> "You said top 300 as in number 1?"

> "Yeah she made number one so why George sent me out here as early as he did so we could snag her first!"

She saw the puzzlement in their eyes. Melanie came to her smiled and kissed her cheek she then spoke,

> "Ready to go baby?"

> "Whenever you are honey!"

> "Well since how you stumped them to a frazzle. I think that we have a party to get ready for?"

Melanie turned to them and cleared her throat,

> "Well I just wanted to come by and tell you guys I gotta get back. I have an awards ceremony to go to."

> "Do us proud honey. Ms. Hawke make sure you look out for her now?"

> "Will do sir"

Melanie closed the door and immediately hugged Brandy who was caught off guard. She hugged her back Brandy sighed and closed her eyes she heard Melanie speak.

> "Thanks for being nice in there?"

> "I was being honest Mel's. You're a phenomenal and yes every club in America is wanting a piece of you!"

> "You were being honest?"

> "Listen Harper you need to understand while I am a detective I help my Gramps with basketball so often I guess I am a recruit. I know ball I know the ins and outs and I know talent when I see it. You blew me away last night when I saw you play I knew I had to sign you not because Gramps told me I knew I needed to sign you because you have more talent than most of the college and professionals I knew I needed you to lead the team to victory!"

She saw utter shock on Melanie's face. Brandy cleared her throat and went to her side of the car Melanie climbed in and started the car she shook her head the blonde next to her never seemed to stop shocking her. She heard Brandy speak

"You ok?"

"Yeah I am I just never heard so much praise about my game coming from somebody other than my friends and coach and Fran's just saying yet again you have me at a loss for words again."

"Well honesty is honesty honey and you might as well get used to it because the minute you hit the court for the Flames and play that first game the praise will come from everybody!"

"Take some getting used too so thanks for being nice to them that means a lot to me. They mean a lot to me."

"Oh don't sweat it besides I love old people."

Melanie found herself chuckling as she guided the car through the swift curves. She oddly found herself at ease which was totally opposite from every other time she had swung through. She smiled as she spoke,

"So dream vacation I believe we are on question 11?"

"Um let's see if say at the tiki bar on the sands of Australia's Islands sounds like a nice vacation. How about you? What would be your dream vacation?"

"I've always wanted to see Australia but my dream vacation would be getting to go to Ireland to see the pub and taste the real Guinness. Plus I would love to see those green fields. They really look beautiful just to see them in person would be so awesome!"

"That sounds like a vacation you just might have to put up with me because just seeing your excitement. I would love to experience that with you plus adding Ireland too my album would be awesome. Favorite music?"

"Album?"

"Oh yeah I keep albums of my vacations."

"Oh well I love all genres of music although country tends to be my go to for relaxation. Rock for my pre game what about you and if you say opera I'm going to cry because so far you are awesome!"

"I'm a huge rock fan but for my wind down I usually listen to alternative I have been known to listen to a few tracks of country and no I don't prefer opera just to fuel your mind."

Melanie nodded in approval as she eased on to the interstate she broke the silence as the lights sped by

"So do you have a big family?"

"No, not really I don't I have a lot of friends that have my back but as far as family I only have my brother and my gramps. How about you?"

"I don't have family other than my granny and she doesn't claim me."

"Well like me I'm sure you have friends that feel more like family than the family does and from where I'm setting I say that is the same thing don't you?"

"I've never thought of it that way but you know that I say it is the same thing so the next question if you had to choose between a cat and a fish which would you choose?"

"A fish on the count. I have a fish I'd rather deal with the aquarium than the litter box."

"I am choosing the fish as well with the same reason the litter box is so lethal."

They both chuckled just as Brandy's phone buzzed to life she looked at it not recognizing the number not knowing where everyone was at the moment she knew she needed to pick it up just so she knew that everything was ok.

"Hello?"

"Ms. Hawke do not forget 6:30 tonight."

"I won't fully plan on attending this event tonight?"

Melanie smiled as she watched Brandy hang the phone up.

"Who was that?"

"Your coach is wanting me to go to this thing tonight. That is why I was relieved when you asked me so I don't go alone hell I don't even know why she wants me to go?"

"Really?"

Melanie smiled because she knew exactly why her coach had invited Brandy so she didn't have to deal with Cyn's cousin.

"Yeah didn't really give me an option."

"Well I'm glad that I know that now because I didn't want to go alone either."

"Won't Cynthia and Sarah be there?"

"Oh yeah but with them being a couple totally makes them the third wheel sometimes!"

Brandy smiled as the city lights came into view. Melanie spoke,

"So dress or tux?"

"Dress baby, I like to glisten and shine sometimes you?"

"Tux for me. I can dress up but hate to wear lace."

"Boxers or lace?"

"Boxers for me. I wear lace on occasion but I love my boxers you?'

"Love my lace, baby."

Melanie licked her lips so aching to know just what lace she wore at that moment. She sputtered as Brandy sighed

"Red or white?"

"What?'

"Wine? Red or white wine?"

"I don't know, never tried it"

Melanie turned into the hotel parking lot Brandy climbed out waited for Melanie to meet her.

"Melanie Brooks, can I be your date for tonight?"

"I said yeah."

Brandy pulled Melanie to and brushed the brunette locks out of her face.

"Melanie Brooks, can I kiss you?"

Melanie all but muttered yes as Brandy lightly kissed her knowing she'd have to have more she pulled back.

"Brandy can you pick me up?"

"Sure!"

Melanie knew she had one question left she sent the message to Brandy's phone. Brandy looked at the message.

> "I know I asked this before but you're so beautiful I want to make sure I can date you?"

Brandy closed her eyes looked at Melanie walked to Melanie smiled and answered yes. Kissed Melanie deep Melanie responded whole heartedly Brandy pulled away.

> "I'll pick you up at 6:00!"

> "Okay baby. Thank you!"

Melanie watched Brandy slung the bag over her shoulder and went through the doors

Melanie smiled as she stood in her tux. She was excited to hang on Brandy's arm she heard her phone buzz and smiled as Brandy let her know she was on her way. She took a double take see tonight was special it would be her coming out event as well. She never wanted to hang on any woman's arm before Brandy she never wanted to dress up till Brandy she didn't know what her friends or team would say. Didn't care all she knew was she wanted Brandy.

Brandy headed to the elevator up to Melanie's apartment as she knocked. Melanie opened the door stood stunned Brandy wore a simple white gown that seemed to hug those thighs. Just enough as well as it encased those beautiful breast with the slit up to her thigh. She wore a diamond studded necklace as well as diamond studs in her ears her hair was up showing off that beautiful neck which Melanie readily wanted to kiss.

> "Damn baby you trying to kill me?"

> "Is it working?"

> "Very well come on we're going to be late!"

THE PARTY CONTINUES

Brandy loved the pinstripe suit Brandy took her arm.

"You look smashing Mel's. I love the suit!"

"Thank you, sexy! That dress looks good on you!"

Melanie opened the door for Brandy as well as the car door.

"So Brandy just so you know my friends will be completely nosey and obnoxious!"

"Good love those kind of friends."

Brandy sent the car in motion. Melanie let her hand ride on Brandy's thigh. Brandy's only thought at that moment was try not to fumble the look. She pulled in the parking lot Brandy parked the car pulled Melanie's mouth on hers Melanie looked into Brandy's eyes smile.

"Come on!"

Melanie climbed out and hurried to open the door for Brandy. She held out her hand for Brandy. Melanie proudly led Brandy in the doors. Brandy felt her heart flip as Melanie led her to the table of loud girls who seemed just like her friends. She smiled as all eyes landed on Melanie who stopped at the table.

"Damn Red Hot!"

"Looking good man who is that sexy beast on your arm?"

"This is Brandy."

"Oh damn you're sure looking fine honey easily stealing the show."

Melanie pulled the chair out for Brandy and set beside her. Brandy smiled and spoke,

"So who's these ladies?"

"Oh my manners the blonde sitting beside you is Cyn my bff. The red head is Tammy and the one by me is Sarah."

"Nice to meet you ladies!"

"You too so Melanie. Totally didn't know you were on our wagon but I must say you're so damn hot not that you're not always hot just damn nice to see you dress up!"

"Sarah you didn't know?"

"Honey none of us did but now that you're out you got any interests?"

Brandy ran a hand down Melanie's thigh as she ran her tongue in Melanie's ear totally sending Melanie in fits. Brandy locked eyes with the girls.

"Hate to tell yall but this sexy being is spoken for she is my girl"

"Like seriously she isn't even on the market for what a second!"

Melanie spoke up,

"Um I was never on the market Brandy had me at hello. She's been my girl will be my girl sorry ladies."

Brandy locked eyes with Melanie who leaned into her ear and whispered,

"You thirsty?"

"Nah not for a beverage but I definitely am for you!"

Melanie slid closer to Brandy and asked

"Really?"

THE PARTY CONTINUES

"Yup!"

About that time the applause erupted bringing Melanie and Brandy to their feet. Brandy saw the coach come to the center of the stage.

"Well thanks everyone this team has brought home the championship as well as hope for a repeat season next year. We sure finished with a bang didn't we?"

Melanie let her hand find Brandy's leg sending Brandy into a throaty moan. Brandy already was wet she never met anyone like Melanie someone who was so timid but so strong someone who made her want so much. Melanie went to her ear.

"I'm so glad you came."

"Me too!"

Melanie came away with four awards Brandy drove to Melanie's apartment climbed out with Melanie.

"I gotta go back tomorrow."

"Tomorrow?"

"Yes baby. I got a job plus gramps wants this finalized as soon as possible."

"Then give me tonight."

Brandy cried out as Melanie rocked her hips. Melanie found herself on the bottom. Brandy took the strap off found Melanie with her tongue. Brandy smiled as Melanie arched for more. Brandy slid her finger in sending Melanie crying out they raced as Brandy found Melanie's lips this time it was slow. Brandy took her time kissing every inch of Melanie. Melanie never felt this. She held Brandy tight sweat pouring. Melanie found Brandy's nipple sending Brandy into a frenzy. They lay holding each other Brandy closed her eyes as Melanie lay on her chest. Brandy knew she would never forget this night.

Melanie awaken with the sun showing she smiled as she rolled over laid her hand on Brandy who lay sleeping. Melanie climbed out of bed as she did Brandy awoke.

"Where are you going?"

"I got class in a couple of hours figured I would grab breakfast."

"Come here!"

Melanie watched as the sheets fell. Melanie loved that tan skin against white sheets. She always thought the tan blonde in white sheets was just for the movies but here she had one in her bed so damn beautiful. Melanie walked to her thanking God. She wanted her. Brandy captured her mouth they both raced. Melanie pulled away.

"Look honey if you keep kissing me like that. I'm going to end up naked and late for class."

Brandy smiled sending Melanie into a chuckle.

"I'll be back Hawke just be here when I get back."

"I'm going nowhere right now."

"Good!"

Brandy laid back down. She sighed, odd she found love thousands of miles away just was her luck though. She climbed out of bed just as her phone rang.

"Yo?"

"Hey chick!"

"Hey, Gwen! What's up?"

"New development on Bradford."

"Really?"

THE PARTY CONTINUES

"Trust me, he's pathetically good don't do anything."

"..."

"What?"

"We sent a crew out."

"Just what he wanted too. I'm telling you to to tell them to stand down Gwen. I'm telling you!"

"Gotta go!"

"Damn!"

Melanie froze,

"Babe you ok?"

Brandy came to her held her close closed her eyes she wanted to lay it all out now.

"That was work Melanie. I work a grueling job. I'm talking I might be gone a month or so at a time!"

"I know you told me plus I know how it works Hawke trust me if I didn't think that we could be together we never would have come together!"

Brandy felt relief wash over her Melanie handed her coffee.

"So can you talk about it?"

"I worked a job before I came here. Four months nabbed a bastard just not the top bastard now he laid bait for some of my crew. I told them not to send them in!"

"Easy baby you told them it's sad that people will die before they learn."

Melanie ran a hand down Brandy's face. Brandy locked eyes.

>"Your mine, Brooks!"

>"So glad you say that cause your mine as well!"

>"I do have to go."

>"Let me walk you to your car."

>"Actually I was hoping you'd drive me to the airport. Keep my car give me a reason to come back."

>"You don't need a reason. Brandy as of last night your my girlfriend as I am your girlfriend. Well come on I'll drive you to the airport."

>"It'll be faster that way and time is an issue here."

>"Totally understand!"

Brandy called gramps as they headed to her car.

>"Yeah princess?"

>"I need the jet."

>"Why?"

>"Baxter's crew is in danger. I need to get there as fast as possible."

>"Ok I'll get things in motion."

>"Thanks Gramps."

Melanie headed to the airport. Brandy laid her hand on her thigh.

>"I'll call you everyday baby know if I don't that I am working."

>"Okay and you know that if I don't that I am in class."

"I'll be back when I can."

"I'll come to you I have fall break coming up in a few weeks so I'll come to you this time!"

Brandy found a piece of paper and a pen she put it by Melanie's phone.

"That's gramps number when you're ready give him a call he will send the jet."

"I don't know?"

"Mel's you are my woman you will."

"Yes ma'am!"

Melanie pulled up in departures she climbed out. Helped Brandy out Melanie kissed her right there in front of everyone and for a second it felt like it was just them. Brandy fully responded both aware of the want that still simmered between them Melanie reluctantly pulled away.

"Call me well around 4 but message me often Hawke!"

"Same for you, Brooks. I'll be watching the game!"

"Alright I'll have to put on a show."

"You do that!"

Melanie kissed her one more time just had to have one more taste to do her. Brandy closed her eyes as Melanie pulled away. Brandy stepped back and watched her walk to her car and head out. Brandy headed to the desk.

"I'm Brandy Hawke. George Hawke sent me…"

"Yes ma'am. He called approximately forty minutes ago wait at gate E12!"

"Thank you"

Brandy headed to the terminal wishing to God that Gwen would have listened to her. If she had maybe there wouldn't be fatalities. Why did she not listen? Why did she hang up the phone? Brandy shook her head yeah Bradford was a bastard. Yeah he had pull but why didn't she just listen? Why so quiet? Well soon she would find out what all the hell was going on and don't think she was going to take it lightly because whatever fatalities they had right now was totally out of ignorance and totally avoidable.

Melanie pulled into the school parking lot everyone was staring at her. She couldn't help but smile sure they smiled at her before but this time it was a little different hell even cheerleader chicks was giving her the nod. She knew there was only one woman that made her ache so she smiled and nodded back tipped her hat and headed to criminology. She smiled as she sat at her table with 5 minutes to spare Cyn came in she was a mess.

"Whew I'm glad to see you."

"What happened?"

"Sarah asked me out."

"So?"

"So I sputtered blurted totally messed up."

"Nah she already knew that about you. I'd say she's still waiting on an answer."

"Oh boy!"

At that moment Sarah came in. Melanie chuckled pulled out her books because the professor followed Sarah in.

"Just chill man everything will be ok."

"How do you know?"

Melanie smiled as flashbacks of last night danced in her mind she spoke.

"I just do have faith."

"I'll try."

Melanie felt her phone buzz she smiled as she pulled it out and saw the message from Brandy.

"Hey!"

"Hey you make the jet?"

"Yeah how about you? Did you make class?"

"Yeah with enough time to help Cyn with a few issues."

"That sound exciting!"

"It is quite interesting. I was remembering my night last night."

"Were you now?"

"Yeah and I already miss you!"

"Miss you too"

"Class is starting. I'll chat later."

"Bye for now Mel's!"

"Bye Hawke!"

Brandy sat back so wishing she could just bring Melanie with her. She felt so alive beside Melanie, her phone rang.

"Yeah?"

"You were right."

"I know I was right."

Brandy took a deep breath sighed and asked the question that would weigh on her.

"How many?"

"3."

"Bradford's cold. I'll be there in an hour."

"Ok so?"

"What?'

"Come on cuz who is she?"

"Someone I hated to leave"

"So serious?"

"Could be I don't know yet please have those files on my desk. This bastard is mine you should have listened to me you knew I was right. Now three lives are lost Gwen. I need to see everything. I've studied this bastard for three years close to two under. He's only getting bolder which means he's growing more dangerous and eventually will get to where nobody is safe."

"I'll have everything on your desk when you get here."

"Thank you! The faster I have everything the faster we get on his ass."

"What was the work for gramps?"

"Nothing major."

"Alright I will get it out of you."

"Not until I want you to know."

Damn it Brandy was so hard headed. Gwen knew it was somebody the fact that she did not rip her ass over last night and chew down her fucking back meant that she had someone.

"Well Gwen. I'm hoping off of here try to take a nap. See you in a few!"

"Okay love you cuz!"

"Love you too!"

Brandy looked at her phone for a minute. Gwen was great but nosey. Brandy smiled whatever her and Melanie had it was between them. Brandy set back closed her eyes knowing she probably would be working late.

Melanie stood gathered her books as Sarah came to her.

"So I never figured you'd be gay."

"Why?"

"Well cause you were always with Paul."

"He's Cyn's cousin."

"Oh so who was your girlfriend."

"Her name is Brandy!"

"She's hot!"

"Yeah she is, isn't she?"

Sarah blushed as Melanie walked a passed her. Sarah blurted out,

"I just wished that I had known I always thought you were beautiful."

Melanie walked up to her and smiled,

> "If it weren't for Brandy you'd never found out. See Brandy brought out the real me. She's special Sarah. Cyn's truly a great person."

> "I know. Just she always stutters."

> "She finds you hot. Have patience she'll come around."

> "I hope so!"

Cyn walked up she exhaled deeply. Melanie bit back a chuckle. She heard Cyn speak,

> "Sarah will you go out with me?"

> "About damn time."

Melanie eased away just as her phone rang.

> "Hey baby!"

> "Hey honey listen I just got word that the case I told you about?"

> "I remember."

> "Three fatalities our own."

> "Damn so you gotta work late?"

> "Yeah nail this bastard. I was hoping to get here faster!"

> "It's okay honey. Do what you got to do I'll be here."

> "I wish you were here with me."

> "I know. I'll be there soon."

> "Can't wait, still message me please?"

> "Same goes for you. I miss you too. Sarah says you're hot."

"Does she know? What does Red Hot think of me?"

"Red Hot thinks you're the hottest woman on the planet is damn lucky you chose her to be your girlfriend. I walked right a passed her than she told me she didn't even know I was gay?"

"Well she wasn't looking too closely."

"You make me feel so special Brandy."

"You are special my kind of special. Don't forget that!"

"I'll message you baby, call me when you can?"

"I will. I miss you!"

"I miss you, bye!"

Melanie headed to her car were she found her coach waiting it wasn't unusual it just wasn't likely since to how the next game was like a scrimmage

"Coach?"

"I needed to see you!"

"Did I miss something?"

"Oh no. I just wanted to see how you are."

"I'm great. Have some homework to do?"

"Can I speak to you?"

"Umm sure."

Melanie put her bag into her car as coach came to her. She wondered what was on the ladies mind what was making that worry line on her face. She noticed the woman had a couple books in her hands.

"What are those coach?"

"Oh just a few books that I wanted to share with you."

"Help with what exactly. I mean I have my future planned out coach. You yourself know. I'm going to play ball. We both know that was my ultimate goal in life."

"I know I just worry about you. Is it ok that I worry about the one woman that I had the privilege of coaching who could really make it all the way!"

"No it's not a bad thing it's just I'm not used to it."

"You really looked good against Richter. Really made me proud. I hope that it's just a sign of things to come."

"You know it."

"You look really good at the banquet so did Ms. Hawke."

"I'm just glad it wasn't Paul."

"I know he is so boring with his insurance talk."

"Totally!"

"You do us proud in L.A. Mel's."

"I do 100 percent wherever I go."

"I know you do just happy that your dreams are coming true if anyone deserves this success it is you."

"I know it's so surreal one minute that is what I'm pushing for and now that I have that coming, what do I push for now?"

THE PARTY CONTINUES

"To leave a legacy, Brooks. That's all any player wants. So I see the blonde left you the German?"

"Oh yeah she had to fly to L.A. this morning said I could keep it."

"Easy Mel's I want you to reach as far as you can go that means with her as well. I always knew with you it would be real."

"Thanks coach. I mean it."

"Just do us proud."

Melanie arced a brow til she heard Cyn and Sarah come up coach gave her a wink and walked off. Cyn spoke,

"Holy shit Mel's!"

"What?"

"That's blondies car."

"Well she is my girlfriend and Cyn she has a name it is Brandy."

"Seriously she is your girlfriend?"

Sarah shook her head as Melanie shook her head then Sarah spoke,

"Dude it was obvious last night Cyn you can't tell me you didn't see the fireworks?"

"No I didn't. I was watching you."

Sarah blushed Melanie sighed,

"Look I got homework so I'll see ya'll around."

"Ok Mel's."

Brandy smiled as her gramps came through with having her black Audi waiting. She climbed in smiled as she saw her bag in the backseat. She headed to the precinct. She wanted to get on the case as soon as possible. No more lives needed to be lost. She pulled into the precinct climbed out just as soon as Baxter pulled up. He looked worse for bare. She waited for him

"Couldn't pick better timing Hawke help me catch this bastard!"

"Going to do my damndest Gwen get what I asked for?"

"Everything that we have."

"Good keep the coffee hot. I'll have something in a couple hours."

"On it we definitely need fresh eyes. Hopefully you find something soon by the way can't miss the glow so who is the chick?"

"Someone special."

"Hawke?"

"Nada chief."

"Come on give me something."

"Ok she is so hot so slick she had me putty in nothing flat."

"Damn."

"Not a word to Gwen. She will not leave me alone I need to focus on the case."

"My word."

THE PARTY CONTINUES

Brandy walked in ignored the catcalls and questions went straight to her office. She saw the pictures on the board and the stacks of files she had to admit that she wasn't expecting that much information but then again she knew that Gwen acknowledged she had messed up. Her phone buzzed to life in her hip pocket.

"Hey had to share."

Brandy saw the photo of Melanie and Duke and she was holding a paper that said *'aced my exam!'* she smiled as she replied *'good job keep it up just know that I do love you and miss you terribly'* she put her phone in her pocket. Took a deep breath exhaled deeply and set in for what she knew would be a long night. She wanted answers and she would have them she wouldn't rest until she did. She went to the board set in to examine the photos. She grimaced at the brutality of the murders she saw Charlie's dead body in a chair hands bound behind him no head. She shook her head knew emotions needed to be in check the other agents had the same. She spoke to herself *'how did they get them like that?'* she put that post it note on the board by the pictures she knew with the amount of torture that the suspects were looking for information. She also knew that their dead bodies was evidence that they were unsuccessful in getting what they wanted. Brandy also knew with Bradford this amount of torture was serious he was looking for something something specific. She closed her eyes she knew Bradford made the calls. He didn't get dirty unless it was personal but FBI agents this was a message one he didn't send himself. She smirked *'I know he is good but how did he get them to cooperate like that I know Charlie wouldn't..'* she knew for the FBI agents to cooperate. That the bastard had something over them something that meant more than life itself if she found out what that was she'd be one step closer to figuring this shit out. Brandy sat down just as Bax came in she saw the despair on his face. Which giving the situation wasn't odd but it was his voice that grabbed her attention.

"Hey boss!"

"Umm…we have a situation!"

"What's going on now?"

"You need to see for yourself."

Brandy walked to the conference room she noticed everyone on the crew was standing there attention to the television. Brandy saw the cruisers everywhere she saw the calling card she cursed another agent abducted. She slammed her hands on the table.

"Who is it now?"

Everyone stared at her she knew she was at a breaking point. She paced ran her hands over her face someone quietly answered.

"William's?"

She closed her eyes she looked at Gwen.

"I told you to call them back. I told you that this was going to happen you happy now?"

Baxter spoke up cleared his throat walked to Brandy.

"You know when brass makes a call we're duly sworn to follow orders."

Brandy looked into his eyes he saw the raw emotion Baxter closed his eyes.

"Look I know these men were your friends they were mine too. The only thing that we can do about it now is catch this bastard."

Brandy gathered her creds and badge.

"Come on we need to go to the scene."

"Hawke?"

"He doesn't keep them over 72 hours we don't have much time."

THE PARTY CONTINUES

"I know."

"Showing us he can outsmart us."

"Yeah."

Baxter loved the way Brandy was on top of her game the bastards didn't stand a chance with the Hawke back. Baxter spoke,

"I'll drive you get with bill down on 72nd see why we don't have that evidence."

"On it."

Baxter caught the keys and followed Brandy out to the SUV he climbed in as Brandy did.

"Glad your back Hawke."

"Me too!"

"You're my best man, you know that right?"

"I do, that's why I'm the one that makes the calls when it comes to Bradford."

"Precisely now what's up with Gwen?"

"I just got pissed she didn't listen to me. I knew we would lose people. I just wished she would have listened to me at least."

Brandy climbed out she saw the yellow tape the cops stood guard. She watched the fresh baby face come too them.

"Detective Hawke, Chief Allen said you'd be here. Crime scene has done been here. Do what you need too?"

"Thanks!"

Brandy stepped under the tape and up the sidewalk to the suburban house. She saw no forced entry.

"Odd no forced entry."

"Not from the front door but there was evidence someone came through the back."

Baxter saw Allen come up the sidewalk.

"Holy hell man it's been a minute."

"Yeah it has wish it was under better circumstances. Come on I'll show you."

They followed Allen to the back door. Brandy studied the broken glass she looked at Bax.

"This was broken from the inside."

"You're sure?"

"Positive look how most of it is outside if it was broken from the outside most of it would be on the inside. The majority would be on the rug and the floor by the door."

"So how did they get in here?"

"Give Hawke a minute she will find it."

"Where were the kids found?"

"Master bedroom."

Brandy went upstairs putting gloves on. She saw the blood she opened the master bedroom door. Visualizing the horror in the kid's eyes. She looked around the bedroom hoping a clue would jump out at her then she saw the window was still up.

"Did the crime scene do the window?"

"They covered every square inch."

Brandy looked out the window thinking like Lila she knew it could be done. She knew under she would have come through this way.

"This is the point of entry."

"Your saying they climbed through the window to subdue a family of six?"

"I'm saying one of them climbed through this window. I don't think the family was home yet. I'd say they subdued the wife and kids first. I know the only thing that would make me choose death would be my kids."

Brandy's eyes got wide as she took the file that Baxter carried. She looked through the photos she came to the pictures of the kids and the wife.

"Sick bastard is using kids."

Brandy looked around the room thinking like her other image thinking what she would do. She looked at the two men.

"There's a team there is no way one man. Hell even two men could pull this off."

She walked passed them down the stairs. She heard Allen speak,

"I need one like her."

"Oh Hawke. Yeah she is one of a kind."

"What say I trade my greenhorn even trade for her you'll get plenty of years out of him?"

"Yeah but with him wet behind the ears. I'd have to train him. Nah I'll keep Hawke!"

Allen laughed as he slapped Bax on the shoulder.

"Damn good to see you sorry it had to be like this."

Baxter heard his phone ring to life.

"Yeah!"

"Another one on 5th and Amsterdam."

"Seriously?"

"Yeah, exactly the same."

"Shit."

Baxter walked to Allen

"We got another one."

Baxter headed to the SUV. Brandy climbed in as Baxter did she didn't have to ask.

"How are we going to get ahead of them Hawke?"

"Just let me visualize this scene two crime scenes are better than one usually gives us something else Gwen call yet?"

"No I'll call Bill!"

Brandy saw the cruisers and ambulances she climbed out found the greenhorn.

"Keep this secure."

"Yes ma'am!"

Brandy put the gloves on. She wasn't prepared for what she saw. The blood was fresh she saw the prints these led out the back way. She went upstairs where she found kids crying.

"Easy, I'm the cop, where is your mom?"

"Mean lady took her."

"Mean lady, can you tell me what she looked like?"

THE PARTY CONTINUES

The little girl nodded as she held her baby brother

"I need medics up here."

She heard Bax come up. Brandy looked him in the eyes.

"I told you second scene gives you evidence. The little girl can describe the leader it's a woman and she had their mother. Think about it Bax we need to narrow our suspect pool. The main thing it's a woman and access to our private information. We just hired a new secretary last month."

"Juanita?"

"Yeah it's a long shot but it makes sense."

"Come on let's go to the precinct check her computer."

Baxter and brandy trekked into the office right up to Juanita's desk.

"Bill get over here ASAP!"

Brandy stood thinking about the evidence then it hit her.

"On her application she put Jack Frank's. He's a no name but he has a brother named Alex Frank's."

"The infamous window sill slipper."

"Makes sense why they are going through second story windows."

"Yeah leaving the kids alive. Taking the women, decapitations the men it's all Alex's signatures."

Brandy cleared her throat.

"How did this not come out before?"

Bill walked through the door his face was red and he was very out of breath. Look at them and spoke,

"It's been crazy today."

"Not telling us anything we don't know."

Brandy spoke in a very stern voice.

"We need this computer gone through looking for breaches anything on Alex Frank's!"

"The window sill slipper?"

"Exactly anything on the recent murdered fbi agents an agents life depends on it now"

"You'll have inside of 30."

Brandy stood looking at the evidence that Bill uncovered. She was shocked Juanita had literally leaked everything to Bradford! Baxter came up behind her.

"Leaking information like this definitely upped her value too Bradford!"

"No wonder he was ahead of us. She fed him everything."

"Who else was she talking to?"

"Alex and Joe."

Billy came to them. Brandy and Baxter saw the concerned looked in his eyes he cleared his throat.

"I need to get my team in here. I need to check all of these computers. I'm pretty sure she put a hack on to feed him our current information."

"Do your thing."

Brandy found the last name on the list. She walked out of the precinct. Baxter on her heels.

"What's up?"

"We got her ass."

"Yeah how?"

"William's is the last name on the list. Now we go now we might be able to save him and his family. He has a pregnant wife, Bax."

"Listen agents…"

Brandy noticed he used the cb.

"Take your earpieces toss them out the windows."

"Chief?"

"Trust me we are a family we got this. Trust your instincts go in quietly we need the element of surprise. William's life is on the line one wrong move one wrong sound he dies we done. Lost enough lives, let's save one got me."

"Yes, sir!"

Baxter pulled up in front of the house down the road.

"Park behind me. Reg, you and your crew take the back. Brandy and I have the front quiet. We don't know what's going on in there we want him alive if at all possible."

"Yes, sir!"

Baxter snuck up the street went under the window he heard her

"Come on tell me?"

"No I told you I don't deal with case files. I just process information into the computer."

Brandy heard the agony. Baxter counted and kicked the door down they saw him bound just like the others. He had lost a lot of blood.

"FREEZE POLICE!"

About that time regs crew came through the back. Brandy called for a bus. As Baxter arrested Juanita. Brandy went to William's he looked into her eyes and whispered,

"My wife…and kids..?"

"We will check on them you worry about getting up and about to see that baby boy."

Brandy watched him nod and Baxter stood there. Patted Brandy on the back as she monitored William's vitals.

"Good job, Hawke!"

They watched the cruisers roll in as well as the ambulances. Allen came out went up to Brandy

"Sure you don't want a change of scenery?"

"Nope I'm good where I'm at. Thanks!"

Baxter watched as the medics ushered everyone out of the way as they called out vitals and relayed the injuries.

"Will he be ok?"

"He will be fine. Thanks to you! You stopped the bleeding in time."

Brandy hurried upstairs where she found the wife and the kids gagged. She went to the wife took the gag off.

"Wills?"

"Is on the way to the hospital."

Brandy looked into her eyes,

"I need medics here ASAP lady in labor."

"Be here in five."

Brandy ushered the kids to Baxter as she ungagged them. The woman was screaming. Brandy was cursing the medics for not being early. The woman pushed and Brandy caught the baby the woman told her to tap the boy on the bottom so she did. She went to the bathroom found a little blue blanket wrapped him up and handed him to his mother. She smiled as the boy wailed the medics came in ushered the lady on the gurney covered her up and headed them down to the waiting ambulance. She heard the girl tell the greenhorn that she needed to call her grandma. She watched as he fumbled with the words. She smiled and bent down in front of the little girl.

"Do you know her number?"

Brandy watched the little girl unfold the paper. Brandy dialed the number she relayed the information to the grandparent and heard the elderly lady say she'd be there in minutes. Brandy smiled as she heard the little boy tell his grandmother the baby was born. She hung up the phone.

"She's coming."

"Come with me. I'll need to talk to your grandmother."

"About dad?"

"Yeah."

"Will he be ok?"

"Yes."

The little boy looked into Brandy's eyes.

"Wills isn't my real dad but he is my dad. Did you catch the bad guys?"

"Yes we did."

"Good cause that's my dad's job."

"He is actually a part of my crew."

"He is?"

"Yeah he is."

About that time she heard a ruckus. Brandy went to the pretty face arguing with an old lady.

"Greenhorn let her through."

The old lady smirked at him. She eyed Brandy.

"What's going on?"

"Wills is hurt. He's fine but the kids need to be with you for a bit."

"Sally!"

"Was in labor when I found her. She had a healthy baby boy!"

"Good looks like you delivered?"

"Yeah they are at St. Baptist on 5th!"

"Thank you!"

Brandy watched her lead the kids to the car. Baxter came up behind her slapped her shoulder.

"It was a good day."

"Yeah it was as good as we are going to get!"

"Sure how often do you get to deliver a baby?"

"Oh shut it. I just happened to be there."

"Sure Brandy you just happen to be everywhere."

Baxter saw the blush, he quickly spoke.

"I was just joking."

"I know just holding that baby made me feel good. We deal with the end of someone's life all the time. It was nice to see the start of life for a change."

"Yeah it is nice. So is Hawke wanting kids?"

"I don't know I might."

"You will be a good mother, Brandy."

"Do you think so?"

"I know so."

Baxter pulled into the parking lot he looked at Brandy.

"You might want to shower before someone thinks you got shot."

"Yeah you're right!"

She climbed out of the car. She showered and went home. Would be grateful for the day that she could come home and kiss Melanie. She climbed in bed and was fast asleep. Brandy awoke to the knock at the door. Brandy arched a brow as she saw Gwen on the other side.

"What a surprise?"

"I came by to tell you that brass is mandating the drill on Thursday."

"Why?"

"Hell I don't know and get this it's only for you."

Just then Brandy's phone rang. Gwen saw the smile she knew the smile but this one was different.

"Hey baby!"

"Hey, how are you?"

"Missing you what are you doing?"

"Cyn doesn't believe that the sexy blonde I spilled jack on is my current girlfriend."

"Oh you bluegrass people."

"I know right but babe if you could kindly verify."

"Yes me and Brooks are an item."

"But"

"See cyn told you baby. I'm sorry if I took you from work."

"Oh no. I actually was getting briefed on a drill Thursday."

"Yuck you got it."

"See that's the thing. I keep seeing your sexy body at random times Brooks."

"Same here honey not much longer."

"I don't know if I can wait Brooks. I need you now."

"Damn!"

"Cyn I know baby the thing is. I have my friends, love Cyn and Sarah. They are like family."

"If I can get them a slot. Will you come earlier?"

"Definitely I miss you babe. I do I just need them as well."

"I understand let me call gramps. I know he needs a center. I'll let you know."

"Thank you, baby!"

"They won't get the bonus. Gramps did that just for you!"

"I'm fine with that."

"Ok then!"

"Hawke?"

"Yeah?"

"I'm seriously falling."

"Don't worry! I will catch you!"

"You better. I get pissed when my heart gets broken."

"So do I Brooks so do I?"

Brandy hung up she turned to find Gwen in total shock.

"You ok cuz?"

"You and the infamous Red Hot? I mean the basketball sensation Red Hot."

"Yeah problem?"

"Hell no! I just now understand the gazes and the being lost in space."

"Shut it, Gwen@"

"Hey, it's perfectly normal!"

"Perfectly normal to lose your shit at random times because you are thinking of one person naked."

"Yup she sure has a number on you."

"Don't I know it? I need to focus on Thursday. How do I manage that when I can't fill out a report without thinking of her?"

"All I know for sure is you have it but you can't lose what you already had so I'd say manage it. Keep busy paperwork is boring anyway."

"I know!"

"Talk about it that might help."

"You want details?"

"That would be nice but I don't want my cousin, one of the best detectives on the planet to lose her job because she can't focus."

"Fine as soon as I laid eyes on her. I was a goner but at that time I didn't know she was Red Hot!"

"Really?"

"Yeah she spilled jack on me."

"Oh shit!"

"She replaced it when I found out. She was Red Hot things changed she didn't believe I was affiliated with the flames gramps had to confirm it anyway. When we went out again she asked me out. I couldn't say no by then I was gone well then she showed me new heights that was it. I was toast!"

"She knows about your job?"

THE PARTY CONTINUES

"Yeah I told her she said she understood the job."

"Damn your lucky!"

"Yeah if I can function like a cop and still be with her. I'll be lucky"

"You will Hawke it's not just a job for you. You eat live breathe it!"

"I did Gwen till I held that baby today till I experienced life with Mel's I realized that what I thought I wanted might not be for me anymore."

"Well we need this diluted for Thursday til you figure out just what you do want."

"I will do my damndest. I need to call gramps."

"Good luck! I'm out!"

"Thank you!"

Brandy sat down and before she got distracted she called gramps.

"Hey kiddo you ok?"

"I'm fine."

"Thinking about the lassie huh?"

"Gramps! I called with a few questions."

"About?"

"Do you still need a sf and a center?"

"Just so happens your clever little plan worked. Cyn and Sarah want aboard."

"See lassie I know how to nab them don't I?"

"I sent clips of their game."

"Chicky if I hadn't seen their game. I wouldn't have wanted them on my team well another set of information. I done signed them 5 minutes ago."

"How?"

"I wasn't born yesterday."

"You're a real piece of work!"

"I told you I would do whatever I had to do to land Red Hot. That is the stipulation she had when she called can't help but say she had me sweating there for a minute. Is she a catch you know?"

"Gramps?"

"Speaking the truth well I got to get off of here Denise is here."

Denise was his in care nurse. Brandy did not like thinking of his failing health she knew the odds and knew the chances her and Denise had a detailed conversation which led to dinner. Brandy sighed as she looked over the list that Gwen left she rolled her eyes as she realized just what the drill was her phone rang.

"Hey!"

"Hey baby!"

"What's up?"

"Be that way soon love."

"So I heard he is a sneaky one."

"He is a sweetheart."

"Yeah!"

"You ok?"

THE PARTY CONTINUES

"Yeah just work!"

"Oh well were packing so I just wanted to let you know I miss you!"

"Miss you too baby!"

Brandy shook her head how was it someone could have a hold on you so much. Brandy didn't know what to do when she felt like this. She went to the gym. She grabbed her bag and headed to her car.

Melanie found herself lost in thought. She had never been so fixated on someone not like she was Brandy. How could someone not like the badge. She bit her lip. She didn't hear Cyn

"Hey Brooks quit daydreaming while the rest of us bust our ass."

"Your just jealous. I landed the hottest woman in town."

"Well no I just want out of here."

"We are about done."

Cyn shook her head as she put the boxes in the back of the truck. Melanie put the vacuum in the back she was coming down just as her phone buzzed. Melanie froze in place she saw Brandy sweaty and those abs Cyn looked over her shoulder.

"Ok now. I am jealous."

"Damn."

"Oh tell Sarah Mel's is hooked for good."

Melanie put that photo as her background photo. She spoke earnestly

"I do believe that I am. I have never felt like this about anyone."

Cyn came to her she tapped her on the shoulder.

"What if she is an axe murder or something?"

Melanie chuckled then spoke

"Highly unlikely!"

"How do you know?"

"Because she told me."

"She can say anything Mel's."

Melanie looked into her eyes pulled up her phone zoomed in on the photo of Brandy's sports bra.

"She's a cop Cyn. See the badge."

"Oh nice proof."

"Oh shut up!"

"Fine as hell."

"Cyn!"

"Wonder if she has a sister?"

"Cyn"

"Wouldn't mind finding out"

"Cyn"

"Just kidding I'm happy for ya!"

"Thanks seriously!"

Melanie smiled as she reminisced about that hot body and hers intertwined she just wanted to be with Brandy she missed being able to hold her.

"Come on lover girl. I'll start this ride out get the love effects under control before you get behind the wheel. I do want to arrive in L.A. in one piece."

"I will but you have to admit it."

"Admit what?"

"You have to admit you'd be doing the same thing if she was your girl."

"I'll hands down admit that but you need to realize we are going to L.A. for a job. We need your 100% game on the court."

"You know I function 100% on the court when it comes to the orange. It's all about the orange but off the court. I will enjoy every second I have to her."

"Good then let's go."

"Let's!"

Brandy knew she passed the drill most of it wasn't thinking she'd done it so much it was more based on experience and skill she stood in front of the brass. She knew they were never satisfied she knew the score to get to be good. She nailed anything that they said now was pure criticism.

"A little slow. Hawke, you okay?"

"I'm fine!"

"You usually score in the high threes, why so low?"

"Figured I would stop to smell the roses."

"What is your outlook when saving lives Hawke?"

"No and you damn well know it you know I'm good at my job!"

"I also know detectives get washed up and wore down we will see."

"Yes we damn well will!"

Brandy grabbed her badge and her piece as she walked out. Roger spoke

"What was that?"

"She was off."

"Sal she still outscored the others by two minutes."

"Still she was off."

"This isn't about the drill is it?"

"It's all about precision."

"No that was about the fact that Brandy dumped you. You are still sore about it."

Roger watched the red head look away and bite her lip.

"Maybe!"

"Maybe you pissed, Hawke off. She is extremely good at her job although pissed off she gets cocky and hard to handle. She has to go under in a few months you better hope she gets calmed down before then because if I lose my number one detective over your personal vendetta you will be lugging boxes at the closest grocery store."

"Well she shouldn't have broken it off!"

"Out get out now!"

"Rog…"

THE PARTY CONTINUES

"Now, out around here we look out for each other because when shit gets real that is all we have. We don't go wishing death on one another get the hell out you are done!"

"I didn't mean it."

"Yes you did! Now if your not off of these premises in ten you and your belongings you will be forcibly removed!"

"Fine!"

Roger watched her walk out. He called Bax

"What up man?"

"Sal Greene."

"Brandy's Sal?"

"Yeah she pissed Brandy off. Baxter I'm talking bad I had to fire Sal over it!"

"Fire her why?"

"Because she made it clear she wanted Brandy harmed. We don't need to lose anyone else or have any loose cannons!"

"That is true, where is Brandy now?"

"I don't know but if I'm a betting man I would say at the gym."

"I'll go talk to her!"

"Thank you!"

Baxter found Brandy at the gym. She was sweaty and built if Bax hadn't known any better he would have made a play but he knew better.

"Cooled off yet?"

"She's just pissed because I cut it off!"

"Yeah she's even more pissed now!"

"Why?"

"Roger had to fire her!"

"What why?"

"Yeah apparently she showed that her intentions was to do bodily harm to you."

Baxter saw the blank look. She did stop and take her gloves off she sat down Bax sat down beside her.

"It changes things when one of us wishes harm."

"Yeah it does Brandy all we have in this line of work is the guys we work with just be careful!"

Brandy looked after him as he left he had sandy brown hair broad shoulders stood every bit of six foot. She oddly thought of him as a gentle giant. She knew he held fury and could back up anything he said but knew he would rather handle things calmly. Her phone buzzed she smiled as she saw Melanie's pic show up.

"Hey baby!"

"Hey how are you doing?"

"Better now!"

"What's wrong?"

"Nothing wish you were here."

"I'm coming sweetheart. I'll be there late tomorrow."

"Good I need my lover."

"Ooh do you now?"

"I do. I know just where you can start with that mouth."

Brandy heard her inhale deeply and get quiet she spoke softly.

"Now hon you go talking like that I get all wet."

"I want you wet and on top of me."

"Same goes Hawke. It's crazy how I miss you."

"I miss you too Brooks!"

"So what are you doing?"

"Oh I was working out."

"Again."

"Yeah I got pissed at my drill today had to work out my anger."

"Now I know what you look like must say I love the view it is a hell of a view."

"Is it?"

"Definitely one I'm going to want to see in person."

"Really?"

"Most definitely my favorite part is the badge have to say I love knowing it is there gives me a reason to look at you and undress you in my mind."

"Undress me?"

"Yeah just like I'm doing now see I know those pink nipples are erect right now just as if I were to slide my tongue in those folds. It taste that sweet honey then well we know where it goes from there."

"Oh do we ever you made a mess of me."

"See that's music to my ears!"

"Is it?"

"Oh most definitely!"

"Well I can't wait for you to get here."

"I can't wait to get there either."

"I'll call you in a few."

Brandy tossed her bag in her car and headed to her house she bought the villa from her dear friend Katie. She had to say she loved the villa she waited til the gates opened. She smiled knew being behind the gates she was safe and secure she tossed the keys to Paul and grabbed her bag she entered the mansion she was met by Maria

"Hey Mar!"

"Hey Brandy, how was today?"

"Horrible Sal is after me."

"I saw that one coming, what are you going to do?"

"Nothing but wait oh and I have a special guest and her friends coming in tomorrow night."

"Special?"

"Let's say she has me seeing her naked while I fill out reports."

"Oh hell that don't happen."

"I know so I need something snazzy up there and this…"

"I got it don't worry but you do need to eat. I don't know anything about your line of work but trust me with that reunion you're going to need stamina."

"Mar!"

"It's true."

"I can handle it."

"Can you with this stuff with Sal?"

"Sal isn't an issue"

"Don't underestimate her she could be an issue just be careful and heed my warning."

"Alright I will."

Her phone buzzed she saw Melanie's number she smiled at Maria who rolled her eyes.

"Go I'll bring it up."

"Thanks. Hey baby"

"Hey you sound better."

"The wonders of being home."

"Tell me about. It's inching closer"

Brandy laid on her bed.

"You driving?"

"No we just switched off Sarah's driving."

"Good because I'm going to tell you something."

"Oh yeah what?"

"Guess where I am?"

"Where?"

"On my bed."

"Are you now doing what?"

"I don't know you tell me."

Melanie heard her moan out. Melanie felt juice flow, she bit her lip, holding back her moan she felt her nipples ache.

"Hawke, that is cold."

"I need you so bad I need your mouth those hands oh and we can't forget,"

"Hawke are you trying to torment me?"

"Baby I'm tormented by the memories of those nights. I think about them from the time I wake up till I fall asleep."

"So do I. I'm sitting here a total wreck from you."

"What are you going to do about it?"

Melanie slid in the back she sat next to the window.

"First off, I'm taking that mouth. Got to have that mouth then I'm going to take my time to notice those rosebuds then I'm going to explore those velvety folds. I'll stay there till you can't possibly go again then I'll see that you do."

She heard Brandy moan, Melanie smiled.

"Damn woman your effect is so damn real."

"Same with you."

Brandy closed her eyes. Melanie closed her eyes they fell asleep. Cyn smiled and shut Mel's phone off.

Brandy awoke she found her phone on the stand and she was covered up. She fell asleep taking heed that she will need energy when Mel arrives.

Melanie stood shocked at the size of the house. Cyn whistled,

"Damn girl!"

Melanie watched as Brandy came out of the door she wore black slacks and white blouse her hair was pinned up Melanie felt want well up inside of her Melanie trekked over to her claimed her mouth brandy responded with everything she had

"Well Mel's we will catch you in the morning"

Cyn watched as mels waved her away

"Fine then I see that's how it is, no appreciation," with a smile she climbed in and headed to the apartment.

Brandy pulled away looked into Melanie's eyes she bit her lip.

"So glad you're here."

"Glad to finally be here."

Brandy took Melanie's hand and was turning to take her in when she heard her name

"Brandy baby, brought you flowers."

Brandy closed her eyes.

"Sal, you know I ended that years ago."

"Well now honey, that's not true."

Brandy turned, eyed the red head, this was what Maria was talking about. This was where she could be powerful.

"Well Hawke."

"Please, I can explain you said you're straight up."

"I am and I'm telling you this isn't cool."

"I did my drills like I told you. Only I didn't tell you I was pissed because she was being cold telling me I didn't do the drills right. I nailed them 3 minutes faster than everyone. Usually I'm ten minutes faster. I pissed her off she hates the fact that I broke it off."

Melanie looked into Brandy's eyes. She saw genuine pain, she looked at the red head. She smiled pulled Brandy to her.

"So let me get this straight this broad came here to intentionally try to get me to break up with you?"

"More than likely, Roger fired her and Bax said she's pissed."

"How do I know you're honest with me?"

"Melanie, you mean everything to me, if it weren't so I'd tell you. Even if it meant heartbreak, you deserve honesty. I stand to lose a whole lot more than I stand to gain."

"Even if it meant me walking away?"

"Even if, like I said you deserve honesty."

"Alright I believe you, don't make me regret it."

Melanie walked passed her in the house. Brandy breathed a sigh of relief locked eyes with Sal.

"Not this time Sal."

"No maybe not but there's always next time."

Brandy watched the red head retreat to her vehicle. Brandy went inside saw Melanie just standing there.

"You ok?"

THE PARTY CONTINUES

"You live here?"

"Yeah I do."

Brandy wanted to pull her close but reframed from it. Melanie folded her arms,

"This is huge, where do I sleep?"

Brandy led her upstairs to her room.

"You can sleep here. I'll take the room over there."

Melanie looked into her eyes.

"You ok?"

"Yeah I'm fine."

Just then her buzzer sounded. She locked eyes with Melanie.

"Well, I got to go."

"I'll be here."

She was pissed. How could Brandy take and replace her so quickly. Oh no she was irreplaceable and she'd make sure the whole damn town understood that. She sat at her kitchen table drawing her plan of action if the tall brunette thought she had won she had another thing coming because the game is just now getting started. She snickered as she thought of just how awesome it would be to see Hawke weak. She's always so strong. She won't be. Not when she loses.

Melanie welcomed the burn, it satisfied her. She set out to do another set of reps she didn't know how someone could live here in a house this big. She wanted to believe Brandy. That's not what had her stay what had her stay was she could read women. She saw the desperation in the red head only after that did she know that Brandy was honest. She smiled knowing she'd made it to L.A. now. She had a new playground. Basketball was her lifeline, it saved her life, now it was her life. She hated the fact she didn't have the comforts of home but that was only temporary. She'd get through the adjustments and excel she had to, not just for her she had a lot of people depending on her. She would do it for Joe and Francine they pulled her out of hell. Joe taught her the fundamentals of the very sport she loved and Fran's showed her just what a mother's love was supposed to feel like. She also wanted to prove to Coach Stella that she didn't waste her time with her. Melanie stood stretched, Brandy found her in the weight room she wanted to moan but just slid up behind her.

"Sexy picture."

Melanie turned and smiled,

"Back so soon!"

"Yeah for now. so what do you want to do?"

Melanie looked in her eyes she brushed the hair out of Brandy's eyes.

"Talk about this Sal chick, who is she?"

Brandy closed her eyes grabbed a water and sat on one of the benches.

"She's an ex of mine."

"I gathered that but why is she out to get you?"

"I don't know jealousy."

"Do I have to worry?"

Brandy took Melanie's hands looked into her eyes,

"No I have had multiple chances before I went to Kentucky. I didn't go there she was just someone to keep me company till there was nothing there but after I went to Kentucky and found you. I have only wanted you."

"Good because I don't want to have to get arrested by my woman for knocking her out."

THE PARTY CONTINUES

Brandy chuckled she pulled Melanie's mouth on hers, kissed her deep. That was all it took both were feasting. Brandy back peddled in to the bedroom on the bed. Melanie tore her shirt off, Brandy fought with Melanie's shorts wasn't long. Brandy cried out as Melanie began the charge. Melanie smiled,

> "Someone was hungry."

> "Feed me!"

Melanie captured her mouth. This time she got lost in the sensation the rise came quick as well as the fall. Brandy took the strap off and brought out her double strap. Melanie felt the sliver of anticipation.

> "Ok."

Brandy smiled as she slid the strap in she engulfed the other side they both gasp as Brandy began. Brandy watched as Melanie's eyes grew dark this time when the charge took place both were hungry hot and racing for the edge. Brandy cried out as she tumbled Melanie followed soon after Brandy lay on the bed, Melanie beside her.

> "It's weird. I'm never like this with women. I usually run them through the mill first, you defy my system."

> "Do I?"

> "Yeah I love it. I'm really falling for you and I'm not sure how I feel about that."

Brandy pulled Melanie back on the strap.

> "This I've never done with anyone. I've never had someone flood my thoughts, with you, you flood my senses. I'm falling for you as well baby and it's coming fast and hard."

Melanie moved her hips sending Brandy in a charge. This time there were no introductions all there was between them a need that was driven them faster on the road of out of control the orgasms hit hard and fast sending both women in a pile on the bed. Neither bothered moving Melanie let her hand stay on brandy's breast she watched as brandy lay there with her eyes closed Melanie began tracing the badge with her finger

"Tell me about this"

Melanie watched brandy's eyes open up

"My badge?"

"Yeah it says clear creek pd this is la"

"It's a long story Mels"

"I don't care I want to hear it"

Brandy looked in her eyes for what seemed like a long time she then took her hand and asked quietly

"Why?"

"Well because I know there's a story and because I want to know everything about you"

Brandy smiled then she sat up

> "I haven't told anyone this there are four of us we have the matching tats clear creek was all male at one time it wasn't a written rule it was known for producing the best of the best well along with that came male egos but we graduated together made a pact that if we wanted to be the best then clear creek was the answer we knew if we made it through clear creek than we were meant for the criminal justice system we knew if we took clear creek on and made it then we had what we needed to take American by storm. we get to clear creek smirk because it seemed aces no one bothered us we stuck together it was when I started climbing up the ranks when I started breaking records the shit

started happening well Stephen was a hotshot felt everything was about him that everyone should bow to him answer to him I made it clear I wasn't there to feed into his fantasy to be a god I was there to do what I had to do to begin my life of serving people well after they all so badly tried to reming me I was a woman and my place was at home legs spread open they walked off well one night I was coming out of the showers we had a late drill and I was late in the showers Stephen pops out with his cronies jumped me they took their turns with slurs and rape at that moment I decide it was do or die if I didn't make a stand then I'd just be another statistic I was tired of statistics I stood tears down my face instead of using my pain to hide I used it to get pissed I knew that I was the one that needed to stand they were laughing only after I had two down did Stephen realize there were six of them one of me and by the time I was done there were none standing laughing I went to my supervisor had too told them what happened and what I did I knew I stood the chance of getting threw out but I wanted them to see I was responsible after that no one treated us like we were whores everyone was treated equal it was Gwen's idea for the tats since we were the ones that liberated clear creek we should have a memorandum"

Brandy saw the tears in Melanie's eyes she looked into Melanie's eyes

"You ok?"

"I'm fine it just hit me hard one rape victim to another"

"You?"

"It was my father if he got drunk enough or the notion at first I didn't realize what was going on my mom stayed so fried all the time she couldn't even tell me my name most of the time see he would and knew if he supplied her with the drugs he had free reign with me she could have cared less the only way I survived was when joe and Francine stepped in and adopted me ball is my lifeline joe saw me sitting on the sidewalk after school one day talked to me took me to his house and told me I didn't have to go back that's the day my life changed he taught me everything I know the only way I can truly repay them all is too succeed"

"Honey you will so my chief his woman plays for the thunder"

"Who is it?"

"Sam Anderson"

"No way Sam?"

"Yeah we should drive out and see them sometime maybe you could practice Bax told me today that Sam was thinking of coming to the flames just because you're on the team"

"What no way if she did we would be so dominating I love her game!"

"Word is she loves your game"

Melanie smiled as she looked in brandy's eyes

"I know its fast I know you know little about me as I do you but I love you its different"

"I know I love you too baby"

THE PARTY CONTINUES

Bradford sat pissed how the hell could one of his very own turn yellow he paced as he waited no way in hell was he going down now no way would he get caught over something so stupid he heard the van approaching the door opened a body landed in front of him the van sped off

"Mikey, Mikey, Mikey what have you done?"

mike sat silent either way he knew he did the right thing and they would know he heard the gun click he smiled content that all it takes is one pebble and one pebble will eventually break a dam and he was one he knew the others felt the same way it was just a matter of time the gun echoed through the night Bradford vowed he was unstoppable and if anyone stepped in his way they would meet the same fate

Brandy awoke to her phone that told her that Bradford had surfaced again Melanie moaned

"Oh baby seriously?"

"Yeah I love you"

"I love you too Cyns coming over later. Maria told me about the court so we are going to play"

"Ok baby do as you wish what's mine is your."

"Really?"

"Yes love this is your home now"

"Umm ok be safe come home to me"

"Always"

Melanie watched as Brandy put her shoes she then put on her uniform top on

"You're sexy in uniform"

"Thanks but I do believe you have me beat"

Brandy stood in front of the evidence photos she heard Baxter behind her

"They found him earlier this morning"

"This is a statement you want bolder this is bolder he's telling us he's in charge that no one will get in his way"

"Tell me what we can do Hawke"

"We need eyes inside"

"Under? You want to infiltrate someone capable of this?"

"Lila has his trust not 100 but damn close"

"If we get someone on his food chain then we will shake out something it's better than what we have now"

"You're crazy"

"It's in my job description"

"I'll give you today to get ready it goes down tomorrow night and Hawke?"

"What?"

"Don't get killed"

"That's always my objective"

"Good"

Brandy stepped outside right in front of Sal. Sal held out a gun

"Well now saves me."

Brandy knocked the gun out of her hand had her on the ground in nothing flat she handcuffed her.

"Well that was sexy"

"Just stop"

"Stop what being in love with you I've tried"

"Well it'll be easy now"

"I don't think so see me kind of–

"What?"

Sal pulled brandy's lips on hers just in time for Melanie to see she stormed off brandy wanted to slap Sal

"You."

Baxter came out just in time to see Brandy get red

"Hawke!"

"She fucking set me up."

"It worked beautifully"

"Go fix it, Hawke. I'll deal with her."

"Let me come, Hawke."

Brandy looked in Gwen's eyes. Gwen could see the hurt.

"Back up is best in these situations."

"She saw the kiss Gwen."

"Did you kiss back?"

"No but…"

"Well let's go."

Gwen climbed in the cruiser brandy hung her head.

"I have to go under tomorrow. Gwen we will try to patch it up if she is pissed. I'll deal with it when I come up"

"But who knows how long that will be."

"Exactly give us time to figure out all of this."

Gwen pulled through the gates just too see Melanie come down the stairs to meet them. Gwen came out first

"Ma'am."

Brandy climbed out Melanie looked into her eyes

"I'm not going to yell, Hawke. I'm not going to show my ass but I will say a kiss is a kiss. Even though I know nine times out of ten it was one sided it still hurts. I'm moving in with Cyn til things cool down."

Brandy looked at Gwen who came around the cruiser to stand in front of Melanie.

"It was one sided Brandy was set up as were you. She was arrested."

"I never said it was over. I just said I'm moving out. I'm no imbicel. I know what Brandy looks like in the heat of the moment. I just feel like maybe we need to let this cool down date have sex bid each other good night kind of thing."

"So do I Melanie. I am about to go under anyway."

"What?"

"Yeah I'm about to pull a stint anyway. I'd feel better knowing you weren't alone."

"You going under?"

"Yeah got the news before she ambushed me."

Melanie ran a hand through her hair. Dammit she didn't want that. She needed Brandy going under there would be no contact. Brandy came to Melanie.

"Look it will be ok."

"How? You're not going to be able to talk to me I need contact, Hawke."

Brandy took off her locket pinned it around Melanie's neck. She placed her lips where her hands touched.

"This is the one thing in my life I care for more than life wear it for me."

"Me?"

"Yes love. I love you. I wanted to slap her."

"She would have to had the chief not showed up."

Melanie looked at Gwen. She was small but built she looked at the name tag.

"Gwen, you're one of the four?"

Gwen looked at Brandy who nodded.

"Yes ma'am"

Melanie went and hugged her then shook her hand.

"I'm Melanie Brooks."

"The red hot everyone's buzzing about?"

"Yeah she is."

Gwen playfully slapped Brandy's shoulder.

"Holding out on me?"

At that moment Cyn pulled up popped out of the vehicle

"Where is that red headed bitch?"

"Arrested."

"Good news saved me from getting arrested you ready Mels?"

"Give me a few minutes."

"Sure."

Cyn eyed Gwen who didn't pay any attention at first then she spoke.

"I'm spoken for."

"Well hell you be fine who ever she be, she is lucky"

"Thanks, Sam says the same thing."

"Sam?"

"Samantha Anderson."

Melanie spoke up.

"I thought?"

"It's complicated."

Brandy spoke up.

"Just have to meet her."

Melanie locked eyes with Cyn.

"She's actually thinking about joining the team."

"Yeah she is. She wants success and it isn't happening at the thunder right now."

"I hope we get her. We would be dominate!"

THE PARTY CONTINUES

"I know I told her that."

Melanie handed Cyn her bag just as she did brandy pulled her too her looked in her eyes Gwen whispered.

"The talk."

"The talk?"

"Cop bizz."

Brandy kissed her deep she moaned when Melanie's hands ran over her back brandy pulled away.

"I don't know how long I will be."

"It's okay."

"No, it's really not."

"I knew this was a possibility before I got involved. Brandy even before I moved down here you were level with me."

Brandy smiled as she took her hands and asked.

"Just no matter what be waiting for me?"

"I will be here."

"I do love you."

"I know. I love you too."

Melanie was headed to Cyn when Brandy came to her.

"Look here?"

Melanie looked at her than at the card.

"What is this?"

"My bank card."

"What do you want me to do with that?"

"You said you wanted your own place. I figured I could help?"

"I have money, Hawke."

"I know."

Melanie saw she was struggling with her control Melanie pulled Brandy to her.

"Look I'll hang on to it if it will make you feel better."

"Yes it would."

"Okay then I will."

Brandy kissed her deep. She knew she would have to let her go. Melanie surprised her with a necklace of her own.

"I know you can't wear it but keep it on you to think of me."

"I will."

"Bye, Hawke."

"Bye, Brooks."

Melanie watched as the ball swished then Sam went to get the rebound.

"32-30 your ball Mels."

"Alright."

Melanie started at the top of the key faked a three and Sam blocked her.

"You got to do better than that Red Hot."

"I'm just getting started."

Melanie juked spun and laid it in.

"Good thing. I'm on your team now."

"It got finalized?"

"Yeah. George called me before you showed up."

"Yes I'm so glad."

Sam smiled as she accepted the hug.

"So how are you doing?"

Melanie knew she meant about Brandy. She ran a hand through her hair shook her head.

"I mean I have dated a lot of girls none of them stick in my mind like she does."

"Brandy's special."

"That a warning."

"I can tell you this much Baxter wouldn't have brought you here if you weren't right for her. He's like her brother."

"I don't know what to do. I'll go insane."

"I know somebody who can keep you busy."

"Sam I'm an honest woman."

Sam busted out laughing shook her head.

"No, no she's with *Vogue!*"

"*Vogue* the magazine?"

"Yeah I think you will fit the part nicely."

"Part?"

Sam was already heading to her house. Melanie ran a hand through her hair.

"Part I'm totally lost what the heck is she talking about?"

Sam came back out on the phone.

"Oh come on. Stella easiest 40 bucks you will earn that's what I like to hear."

Same came up to Melanie she had a twinkle in her eye she walked around Melanie nodding.

"Yeah come on."

"What's going on?"

"You'll see but we got less than twenty."

Melanie shook her head she had her doubts.

"Ok I am so confused."

"That is fine."

Sam told Shelia what she wanted and wouldn't let Melanie look. Melanie just cringed every time she watched a lock of hair fall on the floor. Sam had her put on the white t shirt, leather jacket. She had her put on the jeans. Sam gave her the shoes.

"Hell yeah."

"Now can I look?"

"Sure."

Melanie turned to the mirror her mouth fell open.

THE PARTY CONTINUES

"Like it?"

"Holy hell."

"So?"

"Hell, I love it"

"Good now for the fun part."

Sam led Melanie to the front yard where she was met with cameras.

"What's this?"

Taylor came to Sam. Sam hugged her.

"Girl so glad to see you"

"Same here"

"What did you want Stella seemed urgent?"

"Remember when you called me about needing somebody to fill Zoey's spot?"

"Yeah?"

"Did you fill it?"

"Honey that was last week. Of course we haven't."

"I have someone for you."

"Do you please tell me it's this sexy hunk of flesh?"

"Yeah this is Max."

Melanie shot Sam a look. Sam just winked at her. Melanie rolled her eyes. Taylor sized her up.

"Damn, Sam you sure found me a winner tell me. Is he available?"

"Oh sugar wish I could but he is branded by the Hawke."

Melanie watched Taylor's eyes get wide she smiled.

"Well Max you ready?"

Melanie surprised Sam with her throaty reply,

"Yes miss,"

By the time Melanie was done she was a mixture of excitement and confusion she sat down on the patio not knowing what to do. Sam came out with smoothies. She looked into Melanie's eyes.

"You ok?"

"I just can't get it wrapped into my mind that people want my picture."

"Maxis picture but you make a good one as well."

"I just never knew people would pay for pictures like that."

"Yeah hun it's quite common."

"But it's in a magazine I mean."

"Look hun those pictures are for fans who think your hot. They go home put it up on the wall and do it again."

"No way seriously?"

"Yes Melanie seriously."

Melanie closed her eyes shook her head stood up started pacing.

"Oh boy."

"What?"

"Brandy is going to…"

"Love the fact she don't have to buy a magazine. Since to how she has the real thing."

"But you said…"

"Relax Mels you didn't break any bonds, Hawke really will love the transformation."

"You're sure?"

Sam looked into Melanie's eyes. She could tell the love was there she smiled.

"If Hawke gave you that locket then you could turn green and fat the woman would still love you."

"Gross."

"Its true love."

Melanie sat down closed her eyes.

"Its weird I've had my fair share of the dames lookers but none compare to her. I've never worried about the wrong things, you know doing the wrong things, saying the wrong things. I always am in panic mode about not measuring up."

"Look honey you're a catch. I'd date you if I were single. I'd play but I'm not single. Neither are you quit doubting yourself learn your self-worth. Mels you have a lot to offer a lady."

"I knew that in Kentucky. I'm here the biggest stage there is and I'm a mess."

"Don't think, just do that's how you get through it out here. Do what got you here the rest will fall into place."

"I'm glad you are on the team."

"I want a ring Mels."

"We will bring it home this season."

Brandy sat on the corner she'd been on the street long enough to know who was who. She watched the van pull up. She knew these bastards, where the goons that got Mike. She set her stance out popped Bradford.

"So Lila word is your snow is the best?"

"That's what they tell me as they come and buy more."

"Well I want 5 grams."

Brandy grabbed the bag handed it to him. He poured some on the mirror cut it and tested it. Brandy wished she could have called them in but knew better.

"Well?"

"Good. Real good."

Brandy smiled as she watched Bradford climb in the van and leave. Brandy took her stock and slid through the night as she rounded the bend. She noticed the van turn around and head back. Brandy knew they would come back. She scurried through the woods. She was glad that she had her apartment on the other side of town. She scurried up to the roof and in her window. She knew it was best to not have a vehicle or use the door. She blocked the door and closed the windows. She needed to evaluate how to nab Richard but for time being she needed to bunker down so she took out a deck of cards and set out to play solitaire for a couple of hours.

THE PARTY CONTINUES

Richard needed a fix and damn he needed one bad everyone around him rolling in snow. Here he was clean out he needed to know just where everyone was getting the stuff.

"Hey Richard."

"Hey man where you getting at?"

"Oh chick Lila makes the real shit."

"I need a fix man."

"She's on the corner of Smith and 5th."

Richard was already out the door before he could tell him anything with a shrug. He went back to making his lines. Brandy had done notified Bax. She slid through the night. She knew she needed to be slick. She sat on her stoop heard. Bax signal they were there in play without fail. Richard came to her for a fix he licked his lips as he handed her the money.

"I need some snow."

"Well I have 5 grams. I'm running low need to make some more."

"That works just let me grab it here."

"It was right here."

"Bitch give me something."

"Richard I swear it was right here. Oh whew I found it. It slipped under the table."

She handed him the drug.

"FYI don't call me a bitch. Ill flatten you."

"Whatever."

Brandy heard Baxter shout out orders. She slipped through the night to her apartment she grabbed her bags and waited for Gwen.

"Dammit you feds always lurking on a poor man."

"Well we feds wouldn't be lurking if you poor men didn't buy drugs."

"Well if I tell you who sold it to me, will you let me go?"

"Selling out one of your own. Richard you sure you want to do that?"

"It's Lila the chick said she would flatten me. She fucking sold it to me."

"Did she now."

Baxter got on the radio.

"We need Lila. She resurfaced."

"You're a low down piece of flesh to sell out your own."

"She is over there."

Baxter snickered as he put Richard in the car. He watched as the cruiser blew the horn. He smiled that was Gwen letting him know Brandy was safe. Baxter climbed in the driver side and headed to the precinct.

Gwen watched as Brandy just sat there it generally took an hour or so before she started talking.

"I had him Gwen."

"Who?"

"Bradford."

"Had got loose."

"I know still. I had him."

"Brought you something."

"Oh yeah?"

Gwen handed her the vogue magazine. Brandy saw Melanie on the cover the water was on her skin. She wore shorts. Her hair was shorter. That smile grabbed Brandy right deep inside.

"Damn."

"Yeah, she's been busy."

"Im glad. Where is she?"

"Well?"

Brandy watched Melanie climb out of the bmw. As Sam did Brandy climbed out and pulled Melanie's lips on hers. Melanie responded wholeheartedly.

"I missed you."

"Shhh."

Brandy took her mouth again this time it was slow and brought Melanie's hunger to a peak. Brandy pulled away.

"I got paperwork to do then I'll be over to pick you up."

"I'll be ready."

Brandy hugged Sam so tight.

"Thanks."

"Oh anytime especially now that were team mates."

Brandy's eyes got wide.

"Really?"

"Yeah baby. Gramps is getting a ring this year."

"I hope so."

"He will."

"Well I got to go do a few things be ready."

"Oh honey I will."

Sam came to Melanie she took her hand.

"Come on we need to get you ready."

He was pissed. How the feds dare nab his right hand man and his dealer. The damn feds sticking their noses where they don't belong. He'd get even first time. He made a deal and it satisfied him. Richard knew too damn much. He needed to tie up loose ends. He threw the chair across the room never fails, things go smooth shit goes down.

"Bernice!"

"Yes sir?"

"Get me Harvey."

"Yes sir."

He sat down grabbed a cigar and waited Harvey was his trusty old friend the one Orson he knew he could count on.

"He's on his way sir."

"Thank you."

Brandy smiled as she climbed in her audi and headed out to make up for lost time. She couldn't put into words what Melanie's picture did too her. All she knew she was glad to be back. Even though she knew it was just one of many. She pulled into the villa. She needed to change and clean up.

THE PARTY CONTINUES

"Hey Mar."

"Your back."

"Yeah shortly. I'm going on a hot date."

"Are you now with Ms. Brooks I presume?"

"Yup."

Maria watched her go upstairs to her room. She missed the days with Soph missed that sunny smile those long midnight walks. Soph was her everything and now she had Katie even though she lived far away, they talked frequently. She wiped the tear away as Brandy came down in slacks and a blouse, she noticed the tears.

"You okay?"

"Ah just memories."

"Call Katie."

"She's probably busy."

"Not too busy for you, Mar. Talk it out with her maybe she will come down."

"Maybe, get outta here."

"Yes ma'am."

Brandy sent the car into motion. She smiled as she was eager to be with the one woman that made her feel alive.

Meanwhile that very woman was in fits,

"You sure this is ok?"

"Yup its fine."

Melanie arced a brow shook her head.

"Look this is for Max."

"Yup and if you want to drive her nuts and get a hell of a bout of sex trust me."

"I do trust you it is just out of my element."

"Is it?"

Melanie looked at Cyn.

"Where have you been?"

"Oh me and Sara had to figure things out."

"Oh yall good?"

"Wonderful now what's going on?"

"She down like my outfit."

Melanie shrieked sending everyone in fits.

"Mels it's like at the pub you own that shit. Max is you, just need to believe it."

"I want to be the best thing she has seen in a while."

"Honey no doubt about that."

Sam said and liked behind Melanie. Melanie turned to see Brandy standing there. Melanie blushed as Brandy came to her.

"You ARE the best thing. I've seen in a while."

"Told you Mels."

Melanie sent a smile in their direction. As Brandy led her to the awaiting car then abruptly found her mouth kissing her deeply when she pulled away. Melanie was still in a daze.

"I love you, Melanie."

"I love you too Brandy."

THE PARTY CONTINUES

Melanie enjoyed the food. She enjoyed the music but what made her enjoy it more was the fact that Brandy never left her side. Brandy always had a hand on her thighs that alone made Melanie wet. Brandy went to her ear.

"You ready to leave."

"I'm ready to be with you."

Brandy's eyes grew dark in recognition as the smile on her face grew.

"Alright then."

Brandy led Melanie out to the car and to her bedroom. Melanie tore at Brandy's blouse as soon as they made it to the landing in front of the bedroom. Brandy tore at Melanie's pants they didn't need introductions just each other as soon as Brandy felt relief she cried out sending Melanie into rhythm they raced crying out into each other's neck. Brandy held on tight Melanie smiled and snuggled in. Brandy closed her eyes taking in the moment.

Brandy was awaken when she heard the glass shatter. She grabbed her piece put her finger to her mouth telling. Melanie to be quiet. Brandy came down the stairs she smelled the alcohol before she saw him.

"Freeze police."

"Oh shut up bitch. I know she is here."

"Yeah she is but you see you have a problem. I'm standing between you and her."

"Oh you're nothing I can't handle."

Brandy watched him raise his hand. She moved to the left he missed and stumbled fell on the floor. Brandy had him arrested she slid the sweats on and a t-shirt on as she grabbed her phone she heard a ruckus upstairs. She grabbed her gun and went upstairs she found Sal on Melanie and Melanie's face was almost purple. She pulled Sal off of her and arrested her.

"I need a bus."

She escorted Sal downstairs but the time she had them rallied outside. Baxter showed up he stopped short when he saw Sal.

"What is the charge?"

"Attempted murder."

Baxter saw Melanie come out on a gurney the mask on, the iv ran he looked at the drunk.

"Him."

"Breaking and entering I think he is her father. Someone told him she was here."

Baxter watched as they put Sal in the back of the squad car.

"Welcome back."

"Hell of a wakeup call."

"I'll run his prints figure out who he is. Gwen can have at Sal. She is pissed anyway."

"Why?"

"I don't know."

"Well that's not good."

"Usually isn't. I'll see you at the station. Go check on Mels first."

"I will."

Brandy watched as Baxter left leaving the yard dark. She closed her eyes as Maria came out.

"You ok?"

"Yeah just tired and worried."

THE PARTY CONTINUES

"I called Katie."

"You did?"

"Yeah she said she would make it out here sometime went on about cows and hay."

"Hey at least it is coming. I haven't seen her in a bit myself."

"That's what she said got to go gaga when I told her who you had a date with."

"Did she?"

"Yeah so I'm hopeful."

Brandy trekked upstairs she needed to get dressed and go check on Mels why did she have to hurt Mels.

Gwen was pissed. Sam hadn't called her she usually called and when Bax called she ripped him in pieces. Gwen rolled in to the precinct ready to raise hell til she saw Brandy in distress.

"Hawke you ok?"

"Well no I'm not my house got broken into my girlfriend nearly gets strangled. I went to the hospital but they are not allowing visitors til morning."

Gwen saw Sal in processing. She locked eyes with Brandy.

"That bitch?"

"Choked Mels out."

"who's the drunk?"

Baxter came up behind them and spoke.

"That lovely douche is Harry Wells. Yes Brandy its Mels dad biological sperm donor."

"Sal told him she had too."

"We know that but we need it from her. Brandy I can't let you in there this will only entice her. Gwen it's your show."

"I got this."

Brandy watched as Gwen sat down at the table as they moved Sal into interrogation. Sal didn't say anything at first then she asked.

"Where's Brandy?"

"Hell I don't know what I do know is attempted murder is a hell of a charge."

Brandy tapped the window. Gwen let her eyes get wide.

"Check that, murder is a big charge."

"Murder?"

"Yeah murder if I were you. I would be glad it was me in here rather than Brandy she would shred you too pieces."

"I would love to take my chances."

"Listen lady I'm in no mood for bullshit you help me. I help you that's how this works."

"I know how it works your wanting information. I'm not giving you shit,"

"Fine then go to prison with a cell mate named Wanda who is hungry for new meat."

She watched as that grabbed her attention. Gwen went to the door.

"Wait?"

"You done wasted enough of my time."

"Yes I told him where to find Mels. I just wanted Brandy back. I didn't mean to kill her."

"Well you did and you're going to pay the cost cause you have to remember most of those people you put in there."

"All of this over Hawke geez."

"No this is about you taking an innocent life. You're the only one making it about Brandy."

"Oh but come on now you know how everyone feels about her?"

"No I don't. Why don't you enlighten me?"

"Well you know...I mean-"

"Looks like you're the only one who has a beef."

"Still-"

"Look I am done here."

Gwen walked out of the interrogation room right into Brandy. Gwen shook her head.

"You must have some gold nipples because she is stuck on you."

Brandy looked at Baxter who nodded. Brandy headed out of the precinct. Baxter looked at Gwen.

"What was that about? What's going on with you?"

"Sam, didn't call me last night."

"I say she fell asleep, she has been busy."

"It's just not like her to not call."

Baxter turned saw Sam standing there she was in tears both came to her immediately.

> "I just got back from the hospital. Mels isn't doing to good the doc said she's a fighter that someone drugged her. What's going on?"

Baxter led Sam outside. Sam stood in front of him.

> "I know she is pissed. Bax I fell asleep studying plays."

> "She will get over it. Brandy had a break in last night."

> "Really?"

> "Yeah we got the doers."

> "Good."

Sam rarely came to the station. Baxter didn't want everyone to know his private life he looked in her the eyes. Sam smiled.

> "Date day is coming up."

> "Oh trust me. I know it."

Sam had him against her car. She practically melted feeling him hard.

> "Well why don't you swing by tonight after work? I'll have dinner ready maybe something else."

Baxter felt his member throb.

> "Ok what about Gwen?"

> "I'll work that out but im in no mood for it now"

> "Fine I'll swing by."

> "Good."

THE PARTY CONTINUES

Sam climbed in her car and set it in motion. Bax turned to the back of the building getting himself back in shape. He whistled as he went to his office. Gwen came in closed the door.

"I'm in the dog house huh?"

"Yup you are though. I don't know why."

"Man, I must have said something."

"Must have you, do tend to spout off."

That was a month ago all seemed like a bad dream to Melanie now she sat at a corner booth wishing she was home. She didn't mind going out with Brandy but at this moment seeing her feeling up another woman wasn't her idea of a good time.

"You ok?"

She looked up and saw Gwen and Sam standing there they looked over at Brandy. Gwen cursed.

"Easy baby, come on Mels you can stay with us tonight."

"I'll be out in a minute. I have a few things to deal with first."

Sam watched as Melanie walked up to Brandy. Melanie tapped her on the shoulder.

"What?"

"Well since I don't do the job anymore and since it's not my breast. You are all over here take these back. Honey, you can have her."

"Max?"

Melanie let the tear fall as she walked off. Brandy saw the card and the necklace. Brandy went after her.

"I am sorry."

"Hawke, it doesn't cut it this time. I know you were enjoying that so go ahead go enjoy yourself. I'm done."

"No dammit."

"Too bad you can't have me and expect me to watch you hang on every other woman in the joint. Who looks at you twice? I'm not like that."

"I'm sorry."

"Too late, I'm out of here."

Brandy watched her climb in the car and watched the car take off. Brandy cursed, she should have thought, should have just stayed home. She headed to her car.

"Hawke!"

Brandy saw Baxter headed her way.

"Were you about to drive?"

"Melanie left me."

"Ouch could have figured that out though. You were all over that bucked tooth woman in there."

"Let me drive you home. I'll pick you up to get your car in the morning."

"Ok."

Melanie let the tears fall. She couldn't help it. She didn't understand it if you didn't want to be with someone. Why not just tell them? Why hurt them so badly? Sam spoke,

"It's ok man balls in a few days, be busy."

"I know. I need that."

Busy they were win after win practice after practice. Melanie was a sensation. Sam came up to her after the game.

"So what are you doing tonight?"

"Well I'm not following the team to the local bar so I guess its hotel bound."

"Care if we bunk together?"

"No come on."

Sam followed Melanie into the waiting taxi. They rode silently to the hotel. Sam hurried to the elevator. Melanie right behind her. Melanie looked into her eyes. Sam smiled.

"I think room service is the answer."

"Yeah with some tv."

"You ok?"

"Oh I'm terrific."

"You sure?"

"Yup."

Melanie followed Sam out to their room handed her the key. Melanie sighed a sigh of relief as she set her bag on the table.

"I call the shower."

"I call tv."

Melanie muttered as she began undressing. Sam saw the recent tattoos.

"Nice ink."

"I need more."

"Ink therapy. I've never tried it but some swear by it."

"It works for a bit."

Sam walked to her looked into her eyes.

"Have you tried dating?"

"Hell no."

"Why?"

"For one thing, I still love Brandy and for two she has ruined any chance of anyone measuring up to her."

"Really?"

"I have thought about it so many times. She hurt me so bad. I'd just like to make her feel jealous but…"

"You can you just need to believe in yourself and call Stella and Taylor."

"Oh the modeling thing?"

"Yeah the modeling thing."

Sam came to her. Melanie was naked messaging Stella. Sam smiled as she slid her shirt off Mels casually looked up.

"Whoa Sam?"

"What?"

"You have Gwen."

"Well not at the moment. We kind of had a fight before the road stand."

"Oh-

THE PARTY CONTINUES

"Come on we are both free. Nobody but us need to know right now if it makes you feel comfortable"

Melanie smiled as she pulled Sam to her. Kissed her deep. She grabbed Sam's hips giving Sam the full effect of the strap. Melanie picked Sam up set her on the strap. Sam slumped on to Melanie's mouth cried out. Melanie began moving sending Sam over the edge. Melanie laid her on the bed began again. Sam moved with Melanie they raced both saturated with sweat. They laid beside each other Melanie slid her boxers on. Sam smiled as she came up behind Melanie.

"We good."

Melanie pulled Sam to her looked into her eyes.

"Yeah anytime."

Sam looked into her eyes.

"At least you're more human."

"Yeah at least."

They took the regular season by storm as well as post season conference play was a little different. Melanie caught up with Sam as she headed for the door.

"What's your problem?"

"You are my problem!"

"Me what did I do?"

"It's what you haven't done."

Melanie locked eyes on sums. Melanie dropped her bag walked to Sam.

"I thought it was just a onetime thing?"

"So did I. I mean I find myself aching for another bout sexy."

"What about Gwen?"

"I will come by your place. We can't lose the game tomorrow night. Want me on my game that's the only way."

"Well you know what they say?"

"What?"

"I'll gladly take one for the team."

Sam watched the smile reach her eyes she chuckled punched her arm.

"I'll be there around 9."

"I'll be waiting."

Sam skipped off to her car. Melanie shook her head and walked to her own car where she found Brandy waiting. Melanie smirked slung her bag in the back seat.

"So what do I owe the pleasure?"

"Please stop?"

"Fine I got to go got to view tape any way."

"Can I say something?"

Melanie folded her arms stood in front of Brandy. She watched Sam slowed down.

"Everything good Red Hot?"

"Yeah tell coach. I'll be late viewing tape."

Sam nodded as she rolled her window up. Melanie turned back to Brandy.

"So what do you want?"

"I want you back."

THE PARTY CONTINUES

"You hurt me. I told you I get pissed when I'm hurt."

"I'm sorry."

"You know first. I give you the benefit of the doubt. Second time I told myself its ok for you to cut loose. Third time same girl. I told myself I can't deal with it. You want me back give me time. I still love you but every time I see you I see that."

"Just so you know take it easy with Sam. I've caught Gwen with some of the new hires. Something is going on there"

"I know she told me."

"The game was great."

"We were off."

"You almost had them."

"We will finish the series tomorrow because we will fix what was off."

"I miss you."

"Please I'm sure the brunette buck toothed woman is better."

"You know she's not. I won't excuse my actions and I'll take whatever punishment. I need too. I'm stuck on you anyway. I wanted to see you before I head under again."

"Again?"

"Yeah I went under three weeks ago. I'm in for a big haul this time."

"I do care about you, Hawke. I just need the pain to quit hurting when I see you."

"I'm not going anywhere."

"Be safe come home."

"Always."

Brandy noticed she still wore the necklace. She smiled kissed Melanie on the forehead.

"You take care now."

"I always do."

Melanie climbed in her car and headed out of the parking lot. She headed to her apartment as soon as she was in her apartment door locked she called Sam.

"Hey."

"Why didn't you tell me about Gwen?"

"Because-"

"You helped me."

"Are you suggesting I come over?"

"I'm offering it."

"I'm taking it."

"See you soon."

Melanie smiled as she headed to the shower. She moaned as the heat connected with her aching muscles. She came out of her room just as Sam announced herself. Melanie slipped her shorts on and her t shirt Sam came to her.

"So fresh."

"Well I need food first?"

"So do I that's why I ordered poppy's."

"Poppy's?"

"Oh it's to die for besides I want those hands busy on me."

Melanie smiled as Sam slid on her lap. She made that sound in her throat as she moved her hips.

"You are hungry."

"Then do something about it."

Melanie slid her shorts down. Sam took all of the strap. She let out a satisfying moan. Melanie placed her hands on Sam's hips they raced hard and fast both crying out into each other's neck. Sam hound her mouth feasted arousing Melanie again. Sam pulled away. She smiled as she slid her hand under Melanie's shirt. She felt those erect nipples.

"Thanks Mels."

"I mean here we are naked together both of our women screwing around and both of us know where we belong."

"Isn't that what they call friends with benefits?"

"I don't know I think so?"

Melanie brushed the lock of blond hair behind Sam's ear. She then took her hand found her mouth kissed her slow and steady

"Always Sam."

"Good I don't want to lose you as a friend."

"You won't although if I do go back with Brandy. I am honest."

"I understand. I better use you while I got you."

Melanie smiled as Sam rotated her hips sending Melanie in orgasm. The knock at the door stopped them.

"Poppy's."

Melanie slid her shorts up as Sam adjusted her shirt. Melanie turned the tape on as Sam went to the door. She saw Gwen standing there.

"What Gwen?'

"I'm sorry."

"Not now we are viewing tape. I will be home later."

"Fine I will talk to you then I need to be at the precinct anyway."

She saw the delivery gut walk up. Sam grabbed the food and went to Melanie who lay on the couch her legs open. Sam ran a hand up her thigh. Melanie smiled,

"I'll take food first love."

"i got a little bit of everything"

"Sounds like it has potential."

Sam laid the Styrofoam plates out on Mels coffee table. Sam went to her ear.

"I'm looking for sex all night."

"You told Gwen?"

"I told you. I'm taking advantage while I can."

"Your wish is my command."

After indulging in to some very good food Melanie led Sam to the bedroom.

THE PARTY CONTINUES

"I'm well rested lover, you ready?"

"I'm recharged ready to go."

They got lost into each other all night taking each other to various heights and fell asleep into each other's arms. Melanie grumbled as she woke to the sun.

"Get up sleepy head. We need to be at the coliseum in two hours."

"Good I can sleep for an hour and twenty."

"Nope you promised me sex in a shower this morning."

Melanie looked her way and threw a pillow at her but got up went to her. Melanie saw the scratches.

"Hell!"

"Don't worry. I left my fair share."

Melanie kissed her deep. Sam wrapped her legs around Melanie's waist. Melanie carried her to the shower. Sam started the water as Melanie found her neck. Sam felt satisfaction as Melanie moved her hips.

"You're spoiling me Mels."

"I aim to please."

Sam captured her mouth as the hunger grew, the kiss grew deeper. Melanie moved fast as Sam began racing they cried out in unison. Sam closed her eyes, Melanie smiled.

"So chemistry back on tap?"

Sam looked into her eyes saw the smile

"Oh yeah we got this."

"Good cause the water is cold."

Sam puckered as she stated.

"Well there goes our shower."

"Oh whatever."

Brandy slipped into the game. She had a few hours left wanted to see her one last time. She smiled as she watched Melanie drive the lane and lay it in. She smirked the score was a 30 point difference.

"So you here for the same reason I am?"

"You in the dog house too?"

"Yup."

Brandy shook her head the thing was Gwen still kept testing the girl. Brandy stopped drinking in the bars and nursed a beer at home along with her pride. She came to as the buzzer sounded. Brandy slipped out before Melanie noticed her

"Wait don't you want to see her?"

"I said my piece it'll workout let her celebrate. I got to focus anyway."

Melanie smiled at Sam as the team went wild. Sam came up behind her.

"Congrats MVP!"

"Thanks Anderson."

Sam winked and headed to the locker room. Melanie slipped out of the chaos followed her. Sam spoke,

"My car, 5 minutes lover."

Melanie grabbed her bag and followed Sam down the hall out the side door. Melanie nodded in approval away from the press. They climbed in and Sam headed away from the noise.

"I rented us a condo on the beach northern Cal. We will be out of sight for a day or two. I can't hand you back yet Mels."

"Hey I'm good with it. I'm not ready to deal with drama right now any way."

"Good because baby your mine for a week."

Melanie closed her eyes. Sam drove in silence.

"You ok lover?"

"Yeah enjoying peace and being with you."

"I have to be honest."

"About?"

"Well when you were fouled on the perimeter and Candace hit your breast. I wanted to rip her apart."

"Now sexy. I barely felt it."

"I still saw red."

"Same good for you driving the lane and alley landing on top of you. That's my spot."

Sam blushed as she pulled off the highway. Melanie sat up as Sam pulled into a very expensive condo.

"Damn!"

"Ok this is the deal. I bought this last week. I need solitude."

"I can understand that."

"I'm giving you a key. You're welcome here, too."

Melanie looked into her eyes. Sam handed her a key.

"Friends forever Brooks with or without sex."

"Friends with benefits remember."

Sam kissed her deep then Sam whispered,

"Car sex we haven't tried it yet."

"We need a remote area crazy."

"I'm on it."

Sam drove to the beach. It was late nobody around. Sam tore off her shirt, the windows were black with tint. Sam engulfed the strap as she sat on Melanie's lap. Melanie took Sam's nipple sending her crying out. Sam spoke,

"Oh come on Mels. I need it hot and fast."

Melanie rocked her hips as Sam moved they raced hard and fast. Sam took Melanie's mouth this time she moved slow igniting Melanie's want.

"I need the bed for the rest Sam."

"If you say so baby."

Sam slid in the driver's seat. She pulled in the garage. Melanie was out of the car and in the house. Sam raced her upstairs Melanie lay on the bed when Sam caught her.

"Now kiss me slow."

Sam teased her trailing her tongue along her naval down and around the strap. Melanie bit back, the moan when Sam slid her tongue in deep. Sam smiled when honey rolled on her tongue. Sam watched as Melanie let the sensation wash through her wave after wave. Melanie flipped Sam on the bottom.

"My turn."

THE PARTY CONTINUES

Melanie took the strap off. She let her tongue enter Sam who immediately came.

"Oh baby you deserve this and so much more."

Melanie brought her up gently but when Sam came this time it was hard deep. Melanie then let her tongue travel up to her nipples.

"Oh Mels, baby."

"Easy love easy."

Melanie slid her hotbox on Sam's and began the surge. Sam was delirious with pleasure this time when they raced both moaned and welcomed the want. Melanie picked up the pace as Sam's hand held on.

"Damn."

Melanie cried out as did Sam. They lay spent on the bed. Sam held on tight.

"You're amazing!"

"So are you."

Melanie kissed Sam who sat up. She smiled as she stood slid her sweats on.

"Good thing about this place. We can run around naked and not worry about knocks."

"True very true."

Melanie stood and tested it out. Sam spoke,

"With the strap?"

Melanie walked up to her,

"Are you wanting me to tease you?"

"Yes I told you. I'm using you while I have you."

Melanie slid her strap on came up behind Sam and slid it in.

"Just like this?"

"Oh definitely like this now take me."

Melanie rocked her hips. She felt the sensation just as she took Sam.

"Oh hell yeah…hell yeah!"

Melanie felt herself fall as Sam cried out. Melanie stood there a minute.

That week was one of the last. Melanie had in a while. She sat on her couch watching tv when she had a knock on the door. Melanie put her beer on the table opened the door to Sam. Standing there in a trench coat Sam opened it to reveal nothing underneath. Melanie let her in.

"Look honey I'd love to but I wont screw around and hurt Gwen or you."

"Oh but Mels."

"I respect you and Gwen. I want us friends, we need that."

"I know but Gwen is so she's tap dancing around me."

"Then give her this lap dance baby. Let her know you still want her. She needs it as well as you do."

Sam smiled, let the tear fall, I picked up the trench coat.

"Hey."

Sam turned to Mels.

"What?"

"I love you. You know that right?"

THE PARTY CONTINUES

"Yeah."

Sam went to the door turned one last time to Melanie.

"You are special Mels, thank you."

"Anytime."

Melanie closed her eyes as she heard the door close cursed herself because she needed it but knew it was the right thing to do.

Gwen stood beside Baxter as they arrested William another pillar of the community. Brandy stood in cuffs, still undercover. She yanked her hands away from Gwen.

"Come on Lila. Don't make it hard on yourself your looking at serious time this time."

"What you feds gunning for me or something? I didn't even do anything this time. You all don't leave me alone, this is bullshit."

"Well if you would listen then you wouldn't keep getting arrested."

"I have to make a living 5-0."

Gwen put her in the car. Baxter headed out. Gwen behind him. Brandy closed her eyes as she could finally rest this time. It was risky with all of them cynical. She grimaced at the bruised ribs. A flash back of Bradford kicking her. She smiled not before she connected four times he had bruises of his own the thing that was odd. She had earned his respect. Gwen pulled into the precinct. She let Bax take Will in first then she led Brandy in. Baxter nodded as Brandy felt the cuffs release. She went to the showers. She closed her eyes only to find herself back in the woods. She was sure Bradford had men on her. She had heard their footsteps. She had never felt a feeling like that ever, you know the pitch black someone nab you felling. She was thankful she had made a few hide a ways that's what had saved her she lathered soap over her sore body she didn't come out unscathed this time but one step closer. She stepped out of the shower to an awaiting Gwen.

"Damn cuz those are doozies."

"Yeah earned me some respect."

"I'm glad your back."

Brandy dressed she had a report to file then she could go home and relax.

"So Sam and I made up"

"Good I'm glad."

"Word I'd Mels is lonely."

"I'm not going there Gwen."

Brandy walked out. Leaving Gwen standing there stunned. Brandy sat at her desk after what she had been through. She decided paperwork wasn't that bad.

Melanie pulled into her parking spot. Found herself hurrying inside to make sure she had everything clean. Her phone rang.

"Yo!"

"Hey bestie."

"Can't talk now?"

"Oh really what is going on?"

"Brandy is coming over."

"Oh well, clean the bedroom."

"I am-"

"Relax-"

THE PARTY CONTINUES

"I can't."

"You have been there before."

"I am not the same person I was."

"I'll let you go. Good luck by the way. Totally calling for all the gory details."

"Wouldn't expect anything less."

Melanie had the apartment clean. She sat on the couch her phone rang. She saw the blonde's picture flash on the screen was it odd that at that moment she felt, scared she answered.

"Hey."

"Come on. I'm outside Mels."

Melanie stood on wobbling knees. She felt her heart in her throat. She didn't know what to expect.

"Where are we going?"

"You will find out."

Melanie grabbed her to go bag. She grabbed her keys and locked her door. She saw the Audi sitting beside her car. Melanie felt her nerves come alive as she stepped closer to the Audi. She saw the blonde her anxiety shot through the roof. She took a deep breath and climbed in the passenger seat. Brandy sent the car in motion as Melanie fastened her seat belt. Brandy shot on the freeway. Melanie laid back even though she was a total wreck. She didn't show it. Brandy shot a glance her way then smiled. She knew to keep Melanie she needed to lay it all out so she decided to go to the one place that meant everything to her. Brandy loved Melanie more than life. She figured it was time to show her just how much she meant to her. She smiled as she saw the sign she drove through the small town til she came to a brick house with wide bay windows. Brandy drove in the garage. Melanie sat up.

Brandy climbed out Melanie followed suit once inside. Brandy ran a hand through her hair.

"I know to get you back I need to prove just how much you mean to me. Well this is the very house my life changed in. The ole lady that I went to stay with was my savior."

"Brandy I love you. I just don't like watching other women get your attention."

"I know I have addressed it. I no longer go to bars. I drink at home."

"Sound like a winner."

"Plus I needed to get you alone."

"Oh did you?"

"Oh yeah, I need my partner back."

Melanie came up to Brandy looked into her eyes. She had Brandy against the wall kissed her deep. Melanie made sure Brandy felt all of her. Brandy pulled Melanie's lips back on hers. Brandy took it slow Melanie pulled away.

"So tell me about your adoptive family?"

Brandy still foggy from her effect responded.

"Huh?"

"I want to know about the Brandy that lived here."

"I was rambunctious, sassy, thought the world was against me. Didn't give her an inch. She looked at me and said *'alright young lady you're a tough cookie. I give you that but I'll win this war'* handed me a fresh baked cookie. Helped me with my homework, everyone blasted me that I didn't deserve the nice

THE PARTY CONTINUES

lady that took care of me. They busted my phone. I went home and told her this, she chuckled *'oh sweet pea it's just jealousy they are jealous that they can't have the things that you do have'* but the time that truly won me over was when Adam Brock pinned me under the bleachers. He took me over and over told me. I should feel lucky enough he chose me. The principal didn't believe me. He told practically the whole school. I'll never forget it. I walked in with my tear stained face. She stopped what she was doing came to me right away *'what happened deary?'* I told her what had happened. How he raped me and had everyone laughing at me. How the principal blamed me. I never seen someone so mad. She called Larry, her lawyer, they went to the school. She stood there her hands on my shoulders. She told the principal bishop *'you mean to tell me that my daughter gets raped here and because it's YOUR SON he gets away with it! Please know Mr. Bishop. I'm a very powerful woman right or not I'll go above your head on this. One my child had been through hell and back she doesn't deserve this disgrace and let me tell you something else he comes with in 500 ft. of her ill have both of you wrapped up in court for years. Don't think I won't'* he said *she's a trouble maker. How do I know she didn't entice him* and she smiled as she spoke *because you stupid son of a bitch she is gay'* I had the pleasure of watching his face turn white. He sat there wide eyes. She still stood so calm *'now Larry I want Mr. Bishop brought up on charges against a minor as well as Mr. Locke. I want them to get what they deserve oh and Mr. Bishop, Mr. Locke better find a good attorney because my daughter has the best'* she stood so strong behind me that day. It meant so much to me that I stopped trying to escape started listening to her lessons. I actually turned into who I am now because of her. She made such an impact on my life. I wanted to impact other people in a positive way just like she did me then she got sick. I was there every day making sure she was ok. She gave me the locket you wear, that's why, it means so much when she died. I vowed I'd live life the way she taught me. The thing is I haven't she'd tore my ass over hurting you and I would deserve it. Tell me she taught me better than that. She's right Melanie. I love you so damn much it scares me. I know I came short but I'll spend the rest of my life making it up to you."

"I love you, Hawke. More than anything."

Brandy took a chance pushed Melanie gently on the couch. Brandy pulled her shorts off Melanie slid in Brandy. She heard Brandy sigh Melanie found her mouth. Brandy unleashed her hunger sending Melanie on a full throttle charge. Brandy arched giving Melanie's access to her breast. Melanie smiled as she heightened the race. Brandy sent claws in her back. Melanie knew that meant to speed up. Brandy cried out as Melanie did she had her hands on Brandy's hips. Melanie smiled,

"Feel better."

"Temporarily."

Melanie stood Brandy eyed her. She cleared her throat,

"So Bax told me something."

"About?"

"You and Sam."

"Friends just friends."

"He said she left naked in a trench coat."

THE PARTY CONTINUES

"She did she was asking advice on her and Gwen. Ask Gwen."

"No wonder she was tremendously happy."

Melanie placed a hand on Brandy's chest.

"I did what I did but I was free. I don't cheat when I am not just have to take my word for it."

"I trust you. I was just asking."

"Does it change how you think of me?"

"Hell no."

"Good I already told you the truth."

"I want to show you something."

"Really I don't think anything will measure up to what I just saw."

Brandy shot her a sly smile as she opened the front door and walked to the garage. Melanie smile as she watched those hips move, the blonde hair blowing in the wind. Brandy opened the garage door Melanie stood in utter shock there sitting was a 74 hemi barracuda lime green hood pins.

"Damn baby she is nice."

"She wanted me to find something to keep me busy so I chose cars. I eventually got good enough to fix cars to buy my parts. I think it was at that moment she realized I would be ok."

"Thank you for today brandy it really means a lot."

Brandy tossed her the keys. Melanie looked in her eyes.

"Baby drive us to the beach."

"The beach?"

"Yeah um I want to test the car can't focus on it if I'm driving."

"Sure."

Brandy silently cheered. She had planned the day every minute. She went inside to the very spot she'd wanted to go. She smiled as she grabbed the ring and locked the door as she climbed in her phone rang. She saw Brook's number. She ignored it. She wasn't dealing with anything today.

"Let's go baby."

Melanie eased the car on the highway and took the exit. Brandy had told her to take.

"Pull on the beach baby."

"You're sure?"

"Yeah I'm sure."

Melanie did as she was instructed. Brandy climbed out and opened the door for Melanie. Brandy took a deep breath got down on one knee.

> "Look I know I have come short and I know we are rocky but baby please say yes so I know I have forever to make it up?"

Melanie stood shocked she had thought about everything that could happen today but this had her stunned. She knew she didn't want anyone else that Brandy was hers so she nodded as the tears fell. Brandy slid the big diamond on her hand. Brandy kissed Melanie deep pulled away.

"I do love you Mels. Oh and this sweet ride is yours."

"Mine?"

THE PARTY CONTINUES

Melanie stood stunned.

"Are you sure?"

"Oh most definitely I'm hoping max will pose beside her sometime."

"Really?"

Brandy held Melanie so close she thanked god for having mercy. Melanie stepped back she knew that for this to start on even ground. She needed to tell Brandy everything as well. She knew it was time.

"For me it was different. I prayed for a foster family but I knew they would have lied about what was going on my mom loved her bars and snow. Oh she loved that damn white shit more than she did me. She would beat me if she didn't have a fix so made sure she had the money. He would get so drunk that he wouldn't remember anything. I would see kids playing outside with their parents wondering why I couldn't have a family like that. When I got old enough to know that what they were doing to me was wrong. I stayed after school to talk to Joe about basketball. At first it seemed so hard because they were horrible. I wasn't home to feed their urges when they found out. I was on the basketball team. They started harassing Joe and Francine it got to the point. I told them I was sorry and I would quit so they could be left alone. They both told me hell no that I was deserving of a chance just like every other little girl out here. One day I sat on the sidewalk after practice tears in my eyes. Joe sat down beside me asked me what was wrong. I told him everything I never saw anyone who seemed so mad to hit me but he didn't. He told me to get in his truck. Took me to his house I met Francine and they became my family. One thing you should know Hawke. I want kids. I want to be a good mom. I want to be a good wife, a good family that is important to me."

"Yes we both need that."

Melanie kissed Brandy so deep they didn't see Brooks standing there. Brandy looked her way casually the back her way again.

"Oh hi Brooks."

"Hi Brandy."

"Baby this is Brooks she cleans the house."

"Nice to meet you."

"Nice to meet you. Everything look ok?"

"Looked fine."

"Look I was hoping we could talk."

"Brooks we will talk but right now really isn't a good time. I'm with my woman."

"Oh honey go ahead."

"No I'm not done with my plan."

Melanie looked in Brandy's eyes. She saw the seriousness. Melanie kissed her deep. Brandy responded pulling the kiss deeper. Melanie moaned as Brandy's hands went racing. Melanie chuckled as she watched Brooks trek to her car. Brandy found her neck. Melanie closed her eyes and spoke.

"Honey keep this up. I'll take you right here."

Brandy stood looked into her eyes. She smiled and tossed Melanie the condo key.

"Good choice of words babe."

THE PARTY CONTINUES

Melanie climbed in the car and headed to the condo. Brandy closed her eyes. She wanted time with Melanie just her and Melanie. Brandy didn't display her strength often but the minute the door was closed and locked. She had Melanie on her thighs her tongue exploring her mouth. Melanie felt her strap come off and Brandy closed her eyes when she heard that throaty moan of approval. Brandy moved Melanie's hips with her hands as she moved her hips. She knew Melanie was close when she arced and leaned her head back. Brandy smiled as she watched the orgasm take over the minute it was over. Brandy pinned Melanie against the wall this time she kissed her slow her body hummed so wanting to go now but her mind told her to show Melanie just how much she cared. So Brandy set in to do just that she sent butterfly kisses all over those little places. Melanie never had kissed with the occasional nibble here and there. Melanie cried out unaware you could come from just being kissed. Brandy carried her to the bed. Melanie arced in need opening her legs welcoming Brandy's tongue. Melanie never felt something that felt so right. She opened wanting more Brandy let her tongue dance over those velvety folds. Melanie never knew sex like this. Never knew any of the feelings. She was feeling were real Brandy started her charge letting her tongue lap up those savory juices. Melanie arced again this time when the waves hit they were stronger deeper. Melanie swore it affected her toes. She pulled Brandy up taking her mouth kissing her deep. Brandy could taste her this driving her mad. Melanie smiled,

"My turn."

Brandy looked into her eyes she never knew anyone so eager to touch her. She took Melanie's hand looked at the ring.

"I love you Mels."

"I love you Brandy."

He vowed revenge nobody took his people without paying the price so he set the plan in motion. Kelly was his best hope if her information was good then he would get plenty of revenge. He grinned as he heard her bark orders. He watched as they loaded the bags and nodded in approval she drove out.

Melanie sat beside Brandy as they waited for Gwen and Sam to show up. Brandy kissed Melanie's cheek. That's when she saw Gwen and Sam. She arced brow as Gwen flung her arms.

"Red alert babe. I think they are into it."

"Thanks baby."

Melanie locked eyes with Sam. She saw the tear stains. Brandy arced a brow and cleared her throat.

"Gwen let's take a walk."

"Why?"

"I say so be back baby."

Melanie immediately went to Sam.

"What's going on?"

"She won't stop cheating on me. I can't take it Mels."

"Then go to the condo."

"Will you be there?"

"I'll try to be as a friend. Sam I'm faithful."

"I know I need a friend, my best friend, right now"

Brandy came back on the phone she sounded stern.

"What is going on?"

"Just come and look for yourself."

"On my way."

THE PARTY CONTINUES

Melanie went to Brandy she could tell it was serious. Brandy handed her the keys to the barracuda.

"Take Sam to the condo until I know more."

"Ok baby. I love you, be safe."

Brandy kissed her hard and headed off toward Gwen. Melanie went to the cuda.

"Come on bestie."

Sam smiled as she slid in the car. She loved cuda's.

"Nice car."

"I know she gave it to me."

"Seriously-"

"Yeah-"

"I'm happy for you Mels. Seriously but how do I fix my issue?"

"Honey I don't know."

"I'm going to have to call it. I can't handle finding her in bed with other people."

"People?"

"Yeah it was a guy this time."

"Oh honey."

Melanie pulled into the condo. She pulled in the garage. Sam followed Melanie inside. Sam tossed her purse and slumped on the couch.

"We are stuck her til further notice."

"Yeah that's what Brandy said."

"You know, I'm picturing you naked on me right?"

"Yes as me you but I'm faithful, Sam."

"I know so am I but I'm talking."

Sam kicked her feet up.

"This must be a big case. They haven't called."

"I know she at least messages me."

At that moment Mels phone rang.

"Hey baby."

"Hey how ya'll doing?"

"Oh I'm fine just stomped. Sam's butt at cards. I won the peanuts."

Melanie heard Brandy chuckle.

"Well I'll be late."

"Big one huh?"

"Yeah ya'll just hunker there til I show up."

"We are bored, Hawke."

"I know. Just stay there promise me?"

"Oh we are not going anywhere love. I'll just beat her at 5 card."

"You do that. Love you."

"I love you too."

Melanie cocked a brow Sam's way.

"Ready for some five card stud."

Sam made a noise in her throat. Melanie shook her head with a smile.

They played cards til they ran out of peanuts. Did some quads when Melanie's phone rang.

"Hey baby."

"Hey sexy. I'm going to talk to Gwen for a bit you all ok?"

"Doing quads."

"Sounds fun. I'll see you in a couple of hours."

Melanie's tossed her phone and resumed her place on the mat. Sam spoke,

"So I wonder exactly what this case is about."

"I don't know, why don't I ask her?"

Melanie dialed Brandy's number. She immediately heard Brandy's voice.

"Oh um damn, so Melanie I kind of-"

"I heard you so here's something for you. I have denied my urges but as soon as I get off of here. I'm going to fuck Sam's brains out. Oh and it is best that you stay where you are at. I'm going all night long."

Melanie threw her phone. Sam put her weights down locked eyes with Melanie.

"You're sexy intense Mels?"

"Yup."

Sam watched as Melanie sat on the couch. She sat on her lap. Melanie thought oh shit. Sam felt the strap.

"Come on, we both need sex."

Sam unzipped Melanie's pants and sat on the strap. She moaned in satisfaction. Melanie felt the other side enter her. She couldn't help it. It felt so damn good. Melanie rammed it hard and cried out. Melanie locked eyes with Sam.

"You ok?"

"Come on baby. I don't break. We both need this."

Sam began taking her clothes off. She locked the door. Melanie sat dressed. She smiled as she shook her head.

"You're awful."

"I know, come on, you love me."

Melanie tore her shirt off and her jeans. Melanie moaned as Sam engulfed the strap. Melanie felt Sam's juice roll. She carried Sam to the shower. Sam kissed her deep. Melanie turned the water on. They got lost in the need and the want both cried out in unison, just as the water grew cold.

"Fucking water."

Melanie turned the water off. Sam bent over in front of Melanie gathering her clothes. Melanie moaned in approval slid her strap in Sam arched as Melanie began to plunge. She grabbed Sam's hips and arched herself when her end hit her core.

"Damn woman."

"Fuck me Mels."

Melanie slammed harder biting back her own moan as they raced. Sam let everything go. Melanie herself was fighting the edge. Sam turned to Melanie kissed her deep. Sam pulled back eyed Melanie.

"You're fucking sexy."

"You're horny."

"So very much so but we have to have a break."

THE PARTY CONTINUES

Melanie came up behind her. Sam was standing up. Melanie as easy as she could teased Sam.

"I'm here for you, Anderson."

"Damn you're a fucking drug."

Melanie picked Sam up slide in one last time this time Melanie needed more this time it was. Melanie crying out with Sam. This time it was Melanie vibrating wanting more. She locked eyes with Sam. They both smiled as Melanie slid her shorts on. Sam put her shorts on sitting there. Melanie could see the view.

"Your cold woman."

Melanie motioned her finger for. Sam to come her way. Melanie had Sam against the wall this time Sam knew Melanie was into it. Melanie back pedaled to the bed. Sam grinding sending them both up. Sam lay beside Melanie naked. Melanie lay with her eyes closed.

"You ok?"

"Oh I'm fine you?"

"Yup."

Sam ran a hand down Melanie's chest. Melanie looked into her eyes.

"It's ok baby. We will just give them their medicine."

"Bout damn time. I've missed you, lover."

"Have you now."

Sam startled her hips. She let her strap slide and spoke.

"Since I have you all night. I might as well take advantage."

Melanie heard the knock on the door. She slide her shorts on went to the door. She saw Cyn standing there.

"What's wrong Cyn?"

"Can I come in?"

"Yeah."

"Is Sam here?"

"Why?"

"I need to tell you something."

"Go ahead."

"I saw brandy and Gwen at it."

"Did you?"

"Yeah in a hotel parking lot."

Sam came out of the bedroom. She wore a robe.

"We know Cyn."

"So you two are?"

"Well yeah."

"Oh boy. I just wanted ya'll to know."

"Look Cyn. We have been in check. We still get cheated on. I mean we have casted glances and talked but nothing. They fall short. I'm acting on my urges."

"Don't blame you there."

Melanie let Sam sit on her lap. Cyn blushed and said.

"Well I'm out of here. Oh Sarah and are having a barbeque maybe ya'll should come get away for a while."

THE PARTY CONTINUES

Melanie moved her hips

"What do you say lover? Want some bbq, beer and to talk shop."

"Hell yeah as long as. I can sit on your lap."

"Can she?"

"Of course it's tomorrow around four."

Cyn closed the door. Sam dropped the robe and turned to face Melanie.

"I always need you like right now. I know you fed me but I need more."

Melanie smiled Sam arched against her moaning in pleasure. Melanie captured nipples sending shrills up sums spine. Melanie laid Sam on the couch.

"Oh fuck."

"Oh I'm going too."

Melanie took Sam in every way possible. Sam took Melanie the same way they lay, sedated side by side on the bed. Sam laid curled up into Melanie. Melanie held her tight.

Brandy laid on the bed in the hotel room. Gwen was asleep. She done it again. She shook her head this time. Melanie struck back. Brandy couldn't blame her. She deserved it. She got up slipped her jeans on. She left went to the condo. She found Melanie alone asleep. She let the tear fall, kissed her forehead then left Brandy to her car and headed to the villa.

Sam climbed back on the bed after locking the door. Melanie looked into her eyes.

"Brandy was just here."

"Oh yeah what did she want? What did she say?"

"She said nothing she thinks you were alone. I hide, I want it that way just because we all are at odds. We can still do this as friends. We both needed last night and it was great but we both know where our hearts belong."

Melanie pulled her to her and kissed her forehead she let the tear fall.

"Thank you."

"Oh anytime but I do need to get out of here so this can work."

"I love you crazy girl."

"I love you too."

Melanie walked Sam to the door kissed her deep. Sam held her for a minute then climbed in the taxi. Melanie sat there for a minute on the couch. She ran a hand through her hair she called Stella.

"What's up sexy?"

"I need work."

"Music to my ears. What did you have in mind?"

"Meet me at the address that I sent you. I will tell you then."

"Must be a doozy."

"Oh it is."

Melanie grabbed her bag, her shades and went to the cuda. She tossed the bag in and headed to keep busy.

Brandy lay on her bed wishing. She had just headed home instead of getting drunk. She heard her phone buzz. She saw Melanie's face she sat up.

"Yeah?"

THE PARTY CONTINUES

"Listen I'm headed to northern Cal. Do you still want me to model the car?"

"Of course. Do you want more?"

"Well I was thinking I could…"

"Alright I will unlock it for you."

"Thank you."

"Mels-"

"Stay for the show."

Melanie hung up she smiled as she called Sam.

"Well did I forget something?"

"No but I do need you."

"Honey that usually ends us up in a hot sweaty bout of sex."

Melanie chuckled then grew serious.

"I called Stella. I need work and since you are my costume designer. I can't do it without you."

"Oh hell yeah. Where are you going to be at?"

"I sent you the address."

"I really thank you Sam."

"Just so you know. I'm going to be picturing you naked on top of me."

"Are you going to knock me out of a job?"

"Hell no. I just wanted you to know what would be running through my mind the whole session."

"Good to know crazy girl."

"Well will be on my way."

"See you soon. Oh I invited Brandy."

"Oh you're doing that session today?"

"Yeah and think of her when I do it that way when these photos go out. I will definitely nail it."

"Oh damn that just made me hot."

"See you in a few."

"On my way."

Melanie pulled into the driveway. She leaned against the hood. She styled her hair, wore her leather. She switched her jeans put on her aviators, hands in her pockets. She watched the Audi pull in. Brandy climbed out and froze. Melanie felt her veins heat up. Brandy cocked her head sent her hair down her back giving Melanie the view of her. She closed her door and walked passed Melanie to the garage. Brandy slid the doors up then Melanie watched her close. Her eyes before she turned to Melanie. When she did Melanie fell to those baby blues. Brandy stood in front of Melanie gave her the nod of approval. Brandy knew anything she said wouldn't surface. Melanie smiled.

"You ok?"

"No I'm not but I will be."

Brandy kissed her forehead and went back to her car at that moment. Sam rolled up jumped out. Melanie spoke.

"About time. I was wondering if Stella would show first."

"Ah she is never on time."

Sam looked her hair over, her make up.

"You going with the leather?"

"I don't know, what are you thinking?"

Sam moved her eyebrows. Melanie shot out a laugh.

"Crazy girl."

"I have an idea."

Sam went to the back of Melanie's car pulled out her bag. Thanked god the banquet fit was still in there. She tossed them to Melanie.

"These?"

"Just put them on."

Melanie went in front of the car, slid the jeans on. Melanie was tan she had abs. Sam wiped oil on her tuning out the hum of her body as she stayed professional.

"Now slide this button up on."

"Like this?"

"Yeah."

Melanie sat on the stool as Sam trimmed her hair. She held the bangs to shade her eyes a little. Her back was shaved, Sam hummed low.

"You better love me, it's killing me."

"You know I do."

"I do now, style it."

Melanie stood as Sam styled her hair. Sam turned to Brandy.

"Hey Brandy. Can you move the dodge?"

"Move it where?"

Sam thought she saw the open area in the drive around.

"Over there's a clean view."

Melanie watched Sam grab her bag intentionally bending over in front of Mel or so it seemed. Melanie walked to the dodge leaned over the driver's door. She had a tooth pick in her mouth. She smiled at Brandy, who blushed.

"Thanks little lady."

Brandy felt her whole bossy throb as Melanie held out her hand. Brandy took it and climbed out she ached to talk but couldn't shame hit her hard. Melanie closed the door at that moment Stella pulled in as did a couple other cars. Melanie watched the blonde climb out as well as the camera crew. Stella bustled to Melanie.

"Oh Sam another hit. Okay Taylor get ready. Sam you got it?"

"I do."

"Max it's on."

Melanie looked at the camera as she thought of Brandy, of just how much she wanted the very blonde who wouldn't talk to her. She posed as she was instructed then Stella called Taylor.

"Alright Max. Just pick her up think of taking her to your pad."

Melanie looked into her eyes thinking of Brandy in her bed. Taylor placed a professional hand on Max's that lay on the top of the car.

"Ok good excellent Max. Thank you."

"Anytime."

"So-"

THE PARTY CONTINUES

Taylor lingered. Sam ushered her outta the way. Brandy smiled as she folded her arms. Melanie turned looked out over the yard. Sam came to her.

"You ok?"

"I will be. Thank you for everything."

Sam scooted closer.

"You thanked me last night. I'm out call if you need me."

Melanie smiled.

"I will."

Brandy watched Melanie for a minute then she felt herself walking to the one woman that meant everything to her. She froze when Melanie turned around shirt open.

"I was wondering how long it would take."

"I don't know what to say."

"What about?"

"What happened?"

"Can't change it can we?"

"No but-"

"What's important now Brandy is there enough between us to move forward?"

"I don't know. I feel so ashamed right now. I can't think straight."

Melanie stood handed her her necklace back, her ring back and her keys. She grabbed her bag tossed Brandy the condo keys.

"Let me know when you find out."

"Wait?"

"For what? Brandy all I have done is wait. All I have done is push this off and tell myself today she will tell me. I'm it and mean it. I mean, damn I honestly thought we had it last time."

"At least take the condo key and the car."

"I can't. I have an apartment and a car."

"Please I insist."

Melanie turned to her. Looked her in the eyes.

"I don't know what it takes to keep you. I have been honest with you and faithful I have thought it over. Hell I have people buying my picture so I know it isn't my looks and despite my latest discretion. I know I'm a damn fine mate in bed. I keep trying to add it up. What am I doing wrong for you to do this to me? I still come up short. One thing you need to know is that I love you. Everyone around us knows that I do. Why don't you?"

"I know that you do ok. I had to rescue a baby and I was so excited to get home and tell you about it then Gwen wanted to drink."

"Look I'm going back to Kentucky for a bit. I need to clear my head."

"Take the car and the condo. I owe you that much."

"You owe me a chance to love you."

Melanie took the keys climbed in the car and headed to the condo with tears in her eyes. She needed a break from California. She drove in the night as she pulled in the garage. Sam called,

"Hey."

THE PARTY CONTINUES

"Hey you free?"

"Yeah for a while. What's up?"

"I need a friend Mels."

"So do I come on over?"

Melanie locked the garage and slung her bag on the floor. She grabbed a beer took a draw and shook her head. She saw the head lights and closed her eyes. Sam came in. She was in tears too.

"What happened?"

"Gwen took off with a blonde."

Sam noticed the ring was gone so was the locket. She looked in Melanie's eyes.

"You ok?"

"As good as I'm going to get."

Sam sat on the couch looked at Melanie. Who just stood there.

"You don't seem fine."

"I did the one thing I thought would work but it didn't even phase her. I give up."

Sam got up and walked to her.

"You are amazing Melanie, in bed and you are my best friend. It's her loss if she doesn't see that you have done what you are supposed to."

"I'm leaving Sam back home for a bit."

"Oh-"

"I don't know what else to do. She hurt me so bad."

Sam came up to her went behind her squeezed her tight laid her head on her back.

"I'll miss you."

Melanie closed her eyes sat down on the couch tears in her eyes. Sam froze, she just realized something about seeing Melanie cry. It seemed rare. She sat down knowing she needed to do the right thing.

"Do what you need to Melanie."

"I just need to get away. Find me again."

"Then do it."

Melanie looked into her eyes as the tears rolled.

"Come with me? Sam as a friend, no sex."

"No sex?"

"Seriously-"

"I'm joking Melanie. Yeah I'll come with you."

Melanie smiled a little then took a pull. Sam closed her eyes realizing that this trip would be it. Melanie moved to sit beside her.

"Don't think it doesn't hurt me. It does. I just Brandy…"

"I understand. Remember I'm dealing with Gwen."

Melanie put her beer down looked in Sam's eyes. Began kissing her neck. Sam closed her eyes. Sam stood up.

"Now I'm the last person to tell you no. However I will have to tonight because there might be regrets in the morning. I don't want that to be our last memory together."

THE PARTY CONTINUES

Melanie looked into her eyes. She picked her beer back up.

"Fine then I'll nurse my beer."

"You do that. I'm cashing in."

"You do that."

Brandy kicked herself several times for sending Melanie away. She closed her eyes as her phone came to life. She saw Sam's number.

"Hello?"

"Hi I'm a mutual friend to both of you but since I have known you longer. I'll give you the benefit you broke her heart asshole. I want to break your face. I have never seen her in tears until a while ago. She is shattered."

Brandy heard the click and rubbed her brow. She slung her phone as she laid back down on her bed. She heard the phone ring again but this time she let it go to voicemail. When she knew the voicemail was done. She picked it up.

"Oh and you made her feel like shit today. Couldn't you have simply said she was sexy even if you didn't mean it? She did it for you. You fucking moron now you have her doubting everything about herself. She doesn't think she is worth anything."

Brandy felt her heart sink more and more. She just wanted to crawl under a rock and stay there but a Hawke don't run. They faced it head on. She sat up grabbed her keys and headed to the condo.

Where Melanie was on her fifth beer. She wasn't drunk by any means just feeling nice. She saw the headlights. She checked her appearance and waited for the knock. She opened to find Brandy standing there.

"Oh, it is you."

Brandy watched the door close in her face. She opened it to say her peace, closed the door behind her.

> "I don't have anything to say to you Brandy. I think you covered everything earlier."

> "I fucked up. I just couldn't say anything today for feeling like shit for what I did. You looked stunning, took my breath away, when I climbed in my car. You did more damage than that when you got all dressed up."

> "Little late Hawke. Ok, when I left that hell hole. I made a vow nobody gets to treat me like shit so this little sherade you have going on go tell it. Too the lucky bitch that sits in your bed or her bed where ever the hell you came from."

> "Just so you know. I have no one in my bed tonight."

> "Give it five."

> "Melanie I said I'm sorry."

> "Yeah I've heard that before. Guess what happened you and Gwen were in a hotel parking lot."

> "Who told you?"

> "It doesn't matter does it?"

Brandy sat down shook her head and placed her hands on her knees. She began,

> "Ok I know what it looks like but I didn't do anything all the way with Gwen. When I got a clear enough head I got the hotel room and crashed."

Brandy watched her take a pull of the beer. She still wore the same shirt. Brandy walked over to her told her if words wasn't going to work. She locked eyes with Melanie.

THE PARTY CONTINUES

"Why, why did you do it Brandy?"

"I don't know. It's not an excuse but it is the truth."

Brandy looked in Melanie's eyes. She came in close taking Melanie's mouth. She took all she could get taking Melanie by surprise. Brandy pulled away.

"So are you leaving?"

"I think I need to Hawke. I have fell for you and stood my ground stayed clean just to end up here. I need away to clear my head."

"Well will you at least wear my locket?"

Melanie looked at the locket and the ring.

"I'll wear the locket if I can wear the ring?"

She watched Brandy's eyes light up. She bit her lip in anticipation.

"Please?"

"Yes Hawke."

Melanie closed her eyes as she felt Brandy's hands on her skin. Brandy kissed where her hands touched. She turned around saw a worried look on Brandy's face.

"I know I have failed you Melanie but once this ring is on your hand this time. I vow from now on I'll stay true and sober"

"And I vow if you don't stay true and sober. I'm out for good...forever?"

"Forever."

Brandy let the tears fall as she held Melanie's hands.

"I love you so much only one other person cared so much for me. I never knew I would find someone who would take that much effort. You have such an effect on me."

Melanie ran a hand through her hair catching Brandy's eye. She felt herself heat up. Melanie came in close.

"You going to put it on me?"

"Oh yeah."

Brandy slid the ring on Melanie's finger surprised Melanie by wrapping her arms around Melanie's waist and taking her mouth just as quick and passionate as the kiss was it was over.

"You always have my attention Mels. Yesterday you had me hot, you had me quaking in my shoes. I just didn't feel worthy."

"Brandy I did it all for you."

"I know–"

Melanie kissed her deep so deep Brandy moaned. Melanie slid her hand up Brandy's shirt about that time. Sam came in the kitchen it was when she turned around.

"Oh shit. Sorry guys."

"It's ok, Anderson."

Melanie nipped at Brandy's bottom lip. Brandy looked in her eyes.

"She is here?"

"Yeah Gwen took off with a blonde."

"A blonde?"

"Yeah so I let her stay."

"And nothing?"

THE PARTY CONTINUES

Sam got red. She stood in front of Brandy.

> "What people can't just be friends now? Melanie's is my best friend. Yes every time. I have an issue. I run to her. I've never had a friend that had been honest so true don't even try to say. She fell short. She hasn't."

> "I was just asking."

> "Well you got answered. Go on crazy girl it's all good."

> "Better be."

Brandy hugged Melanie tight. Melanie closed her eyes. She finally had Brandy back. She finally felt complete. She breathed a sigh of relief. Brandy sat up looked in Melanie's eyes.

> "What if we took that trip to Kentucky restore? What has been damaged get to know each other again? Besides I have a few friends there I haven't seen in a while."

> "You want to go to Kentucky with me?"

> "Yeah I do."

> "What about work?"

> "I will take the week or so off. I have it coming."

> "Alright then."

Melanie kissed her deep. She smiled as the sun came up.

> "Well looks like we have a long day."

> "Yeah I'll go talk to Bax. I'll be back."

> "Better be."

> "Uh honey. I will be. I'm not losing you again."

Melanie moved her hips enough to get a smile out of Brandy.

"i love it when you do that"

Melanie smiled as she pulled away.

"I'll pack. Be ready when you get back."

"Good."

Melanie walked her to her car. Brandy kissed her again.

"I got so lucky with you."

"Just come back baby"

"I will."

Melanie went back inside to find Sam sitting on the couch. Melanie closed the door. Sam spoke,

"I'm glad it worked out."

"I didn't give in hon."

"I know. I heard."

"You going to be ok?"

"Oh yeah. I'll miss you but I will be ok."

Melanie grabbed her bag was gathering her clothes when Sam came up behind her.

"I am going to miss you."

"I do have a phone."

"I don't know if that's a good idea. I'll call you all the time drive you nuts."

"Well you can call me just not all the time. Message me most of the time crazy girl."

"I will want to."

"I know."

Melanie looked into her eyes. Brushed the blonde locks out of her face.

"Honey I'm going to always be your friend."

"I know. It's just I have never had anyone treat me the way you have sexually."

"I know babe but we both knew this would happen. Gwen gets her head out of her ass. Talk to her hell I will about it. She might do things better."

"That's it. She has to get her head out of her ass."

"Well that's when you get dressed up. Find a woman to hang on all night. Make sure Gwen is there."

"Would it work?"

"If she cares for you remotely as close as I do. It will."

Sam hugged Melanie.

"Thank you."

"Let me know how it goes."

Melanie scurried collecting all of her stuff. She hoped the trip with Brandy would knock off the edge. Get them back the way they were or at least close. She smiled as she thought of Brandy standing there gun cocked. Her disheveled hair loose encasing that tan body. Melanie loved that woman. She loved her more than anything. She turned and saw Brandy standing there arms folded.

Oh hey."

"You were in thought."

"About you."

Brandy had to smile as she took the bag from Melanie.

"You ready?"

"Yeah I have a request though."

"And what would that be?"

"Can we take the cuda?"

"Of course."

Melanie went to the garage door. She pulled the cuda out and Brandy pulled her car in. Brandy came to Melanie as the garage door went down. She kissed Melanie so deep. They didn't hear Gwen pull up. Brandy pulled up as Gwen walked up to them.

"Tell me it's not true?"

"What?"

"That you are taking off in the middle of the investigation to be with this-"

"You listen to me now this is my fiancé. I will not have you talk like that and I am privileged that she accepted me back. Baxter said I was ok to take off. He didn't need me right now said I needed a break anyway. If there was a threat I wouldn't. Things are calm and I need time with her. To show her she is the most amazing woman I've been with. If you would take the time to be with Sam you would know she is too."

"I can't believe it. You believe them."

"Yeah I do. I came here as you suggested they were not together. It doesn't matter, suck it up. They are friends. I trust them. What ever happened I can't be like you and think it's awful when we were the reason they were together. Fess up man you need to trust them too."

"Yeah right-"

Brandy didn't use force often but when she grabbed Gwen's collar. She had her attention.

> "Quit just quit. I don't care what they did when we broke up. I don't care. I love Melanie and I have come short more than once so she deserved better. Now you do what you do but I'm choosing Melanie and Sam."

She sent Gwen back a couple feet climbed in the car. Melanie followed suit. Brandy sent the car out in a haste. Melanie set there nervous.

> "Don't be nervous dove. I'm not mad at you. I am mad that I doubted you."

> "It's all over. Can we move forward from this?"

Brandy smiled looked at her and spoke.

> "Yes, yes we can."

> "Good."

That week was exactly what they needed. Melanie smiled as they headed back having Brandy all to herself be special. Sitting with her on the river bank just the sound of the birds and the running water was so relaxing.

> "You ok princess?"

> "Oh I'm fine."

> "I see that smile. You must be thinking of that mini lobster that grabbed my toe."

> "It was a craw dad sexy."

> "You say what you say that lobster had it out for me."

> "Oh right, just waiting for Hawke's foot to nab."

Melanie chuckled as Brandy shot her a look. She loved that laugh that smile. She felt her heart flip. Melanie looked her way.

"You ok?"

"Oh yeah. Just thinking about getting you back before Gramps tans my hide"

"Oh he wouldn't do that."

"Don't be so sure. Mels he's old but can still kick my ass."

"I love him so much."

"Yeah so do I."

Brandy took the exit south to southern Cali. She was glad that she would have Melanie back. Unfortunately that meant she was back and that she was closer to the big show down. Meaning a long stint under.

Melanie stood on the court. She had just got the clearance to start her regimens. She held the ball in her hand. Felt good to squeeze the orange. She had exercised and tested her ankles by jumping so she went to the top of the key and watched the ball go through the net. She began a series that was so natural it felt like it was a part of her.

Brandy found her sweaty and in smiles. She loved watching Melanie on the court. Enjoyed watching her just be free when Melanie played people. Watched as she walked on the court smiling.

"I see Red Hot is back."

"Full force baby!"

"Good I can't wait to see her in action."

"Oh honey, you will see me, just get me home first."

THE PARTY CONTINUES

Brandy chuckled as they headed out to the car. Brandy's world went black. Melanie felt the gun in the small of her back.

"Do as I say and I won't hurt you, at least not yet."

Melanie closed her eyes said a prayer and watched her world go black.

Brandy woke up no sign of Melanie. She grimaced at the bump on her head. She pulled out her phone and called Baxter.

"What's up, Hawke?"

"Melanie's been abducted."

"What?"

"I'm serious Bax. I have a huge as headache when I woke up. She was gone"

"Ok calm down. I'll corral everybody, you just stay put."

"I'm going to do some work of my own."

Brandy sat on the step as she called pap.

"Hey princess."

"Gramps I need you at the practice facility now. I need surveillance footage of the last twenty. Melanie has been abducted and I need to get her back."

"Abducted?"

"Seriously you going to help me?"

"I'm on my way. Are you ok?"

"I'm fine other than a huge headache."

"We will get her back."

"We have too. I plan on marrying her."

"See you in a few minutes."

Brandy felt so helpless. She watched the first patrol car pull up. Saw Gwen hop out and come to her. They hadn't spoke since Brandy got back. Gwen cleared her throat and spoke.

"Look you were right. I did what you said and we got back together. Right now I know that Melanie is out there somewhere. Counting on us and I won't let her down. I need to thank her. Sam told me what she did for me so that out of the way did you see anything?"

"Didn't have a chance to. Pap is coming. He has surveillance."

"Good we will get her back."

"Can't fight what you can't see Gwen."

"That means he knows that you would have made him."

Gwen was standing by Brandy when Baxter and pap showed up. Baxter shouted orders to the crime scene unit as he did. He made sure that they knew she was one of them. He came to Brandy.

"See anything."

"No they got me as soon as I opened the door. Like I told Gwen. I can't fight what I can't see."

"Come on princess. I'll take you to the tech room."

"Ok Bax you coming?"

"Gwen you got this?"

"I sure do."

Brandy kept watching the tape. Whoever it was wore black approximately 180 led them to the awaiting sedan.

"Bill may be able to get the plates."

"I'll call him."

Brandy's heart fell after watching Melanie be hauled off. She cursed just as Baxter got off the phone with Bill.

"He is on his way. We will get her back."

Melanie woke up. She sat in a room with nothing but a mattress and a bucket. She saw the markings on the wall one etched out the word *hell* another one said *pray*. She didn't bother to move wouldn't do any good just feed into their fantasy. She closed her eyes again an began to pray as she did. She heard the door open. She heard the plate connect with the floor then she heard the door close. She saw the beans and the bread. She didn't dare eat it the last thing she wanted was to die.

"Might want to eat doll face keep that energy up. Don't worry poison is the easy way to kill if I wanted you dead. I would have done killed you."

Melanie felt the chill climb up her spine. She ate as she was told. She heard the feet come up the steps. She saw the masked man grab the plate, turn and leave.

"Now I want you to undress."

Melanie did what was asked of her, no complaints. She heard the approval in the man's voice.

"Now I want you to go to the mattress."

He watched as she complied. He heard Gus call his turn.

"Hell no that's not how this works. I told you before. I'm the boss. She has done what was asked of her. I get to claim her"

"How the hell is that fair?"

The leader punched him in the mouth. Eyed the other man.

"Because I say it is."

He shut the camera off. Glared at them drew his gun out.

"Turn it on. I'll shoot all of you."

He climbed the stairs opened the door locked it. He could see fear in her eyes. She watched him shut the camera off and come to her. He kissed her then whispered in her ear.

"If we don't they will kill you faster than I will."

Melanie opened her legs. She let him enter. He was gentle. Well as gentle as she should have expected. She grimaced at the pain. He watched as she closed her eyes then he let himself go. Melanie looked into his eyes he went to her ear.

"You are mine!"

Melanie sat in the corner praying Brandy would come and rescue her. Daniel got dressed came to Melanie.

"Just do as you're told."

Melanie watched him turn the camera on and leave. She heard the cheers, rolled her eyes as she sat there. She heard his voice boom.

"You can get dressed now."

She complied like she was told. She was good at that. This was nothing surely wasn't something she wasn't used to.

David came in from a supply run just to see that they had picked up his sisters woman and he needed to keep up pace. He watched as Gus was having his fun his stomach turned but what was he. He couldn't let it go as she was different when Gus came out. He knocked him out as he locked eyes with Melanie. Who held a bloody lip and a black eye.

"If you so much as harm her again you will face me."

Daniel came to him he was built and always thinking he could out do David. David locked eyes with him.

THE PARTY CONTINUES

"Got a problem, Daniel?"

"As a matter of fact I do. You see I laid claim on her so she is mine."

"I'm the boss and I can claim any one. I see. I see her, l like her, she is mine."

David looked at all of them he was pissed.

"Damn boss what is your deal?"

"My deal is this woman has done everything that we have asked of her yet she still gets punished. Hell no. I like her, she is mine."

"Fine."

Daniel knew with David on supply runs. He could have his way and he would dammit.

Brandy paced she wished like hell there was something she could do. Just a fucking bread crumb then Bax came in.

"I got something or maybe I got nothing. It's worth a shot. Down south beach way the local police department got one. Robert pine in custody quite a character. Oh and get this he is a big amigos affiliate. Want to go chat?"

"Hell yeah I do?"

"Good lets go."

He was pissed his empire was falling like dominos. Who the hell picked these damn dumbasses? He had to set his foot down and only go with the people he fully trusted. First he had to go check his little enterprise. David's phone rang. He knew the voice his skin crawled as he was being told the boss was coming. He didn't want to leave Daniel alone with her but he didn't have a choice.

"Boys lets go out to the beach. Grab women, boss is coming.'

"Daniel's not coming?"

"Think the boss will approve of this setup?"

"Oh shit no."

"Let's go while he can be the bitch for now/"

"Sure."

The minute the vehicle pulled out. He shut the cameras off, locked the door.

"Well baby let's have a go."

He pulled Melanie under him. He loved the feeling. He rocked his hips enjoying himself. He looked into her eyes. Melanie arched as she knew to do. She got on her knees as he demanded. She bit her lip as he hammered it home. She heard him cry out. She herself let the feeling pass. He rolled over looked into her eyes.

"You obedient swan. Let me bring you up?"

Melanie felt his tongue enter her. She thought of Brandy. She wanted to live what else she to do was. She placed her hand on his head his tongue reached her center. She felt the sensation wash over her. He smiled as he tasted the honey. He smiled until she saw him. He cleared his throat. Daniel felt himself get hard again. He inserted from behind. Oh she was so tight he felt himself go just as he came. He heard the door open. He zipped his pants up and came out to find David standing there.

"So this is you cleaning huh?"

"No this is me finding pleasure with the lady."

"You're the best at finding women. The boss loves so go find them and if you don't. I don't have to tell you what will happen to all of us."

THE PARTY CONTINUES

"Yes boss."

David came in to find Melanie just sitting there naked. He handed her her clothes and spoke.

"Now listen to me. No questions just do like you have been. I need you to stay in that closet for now. I will come and get you when I can."

Melanie went to the closet. She looked into his eyes.

"Just do as you're told, please be quiet."

"Do as I am told. Did not help me with that bastard did it?"

"I'm sorry about that."

"I don't understand why you are so nice?"

"I can't afford to be too often just listen to me when I am/"

David locked the closet door back and cleaned the house. Just as the bastard showed up. David had the camera showing no one.

"No women?"

"No killed the last one. Boys out now."

"Not you?"

"I wanted the house in a welcoming state for when they come in."

"Good I want to see these women when they come in. You know what I like."

"Yes sir."

"They better be divine."

"They will be sir."

"Good I haven't had sex in a year. These rocks need off."

"I told them south beach."

"Tan meat good thinking. Call me when they come in."

"Will do sir."

He watched him leave waited a few minutes then went to the room. Melanie heard the lock. Melanie watched him.

"We need to move you."

"Okay."

David helped her to the back of the house upstairs to the attic. She watched him leave and come back with blankets and books.

"I'll be up in a few. No one comes up here. You are safe here. Just be quiet."

David fixed the cameras and waited the arrival of the beasts. He heard the screams as he heard the laughs. Watched them herd them in. David checked them had the room ready put them in the room. They came down.

"Where did she go?"

"What can I say? I have a bag of steel. Snapped her neck, the boss told me to make sure he had a divine collection. You ibices ruined this bunch go get more."

"Fine what are you going to do?"

"You bruised these women. That is going to piss him off. I'm going to save your asses."

"Oh hell we forgot to knock them out."

"Well don't forget this time. Do it right? We are already chancing it with you all not doing your jobs."

Daniel knew he hid her somewhere and he would find her. He didn't care about ratting him out or anything he just loved her feel. He found Melanie curled up in a blanket. She locked eyes with him he pulled her mouth to his found her hot and inviting. Melanie knew to keep safe. She had to comply. He charged this time. Daniel watched as she cried out in pain. He smiled as he muffled his own moan. He went to her ear.

"Show me you want me."

Melanie tightened around him with dealing with her past. She knew what he was wanting and knew that she needed to do. What he said he rushed this time sending shock waves through him. She bit her lip blocking out the pain blocking out everything. She just thought of Brandy and how she wanted to see her again. She heard him cry out. Melanie watched him dress. She closed her eyes and prayed for Brandy. She heard him say.

"Just be quiet. This will work."

Brandy sat across from a slime. She just got the vibe.

"So bob what is it you do for a living?"

"I'm not telling you."

"Oh I think you will."

"I'm not stupid lady. There's always someone above someone else. I'm no snitch."

"No even though you are not saying anything the boys and your boss out there don't know what you are saying. I'd say there is a nice price or whoever knocks you off."

About that time, Baxter knocked on the window. Brandy came out. Baxter looked into her eyes.

"She is alive."

"How do you know?"

"Because David just sent us proof of life."

"David as in David Hawke?"

"Yeah that with a word."

"What was the word?"

"Tequila."

"He is in trouble. He is sending out an S.O.S."

"How do you know?"

"We have worked together long enough. We have keywords."

They heard the ruckus as the officer's brought in 3 men. They identified one from the video.

"That is the same guy. Gwen have at him."

"Yes sir?"

They watched through the glass as Gwen entered.

"Oh hey sexy lady."

"Hey I have some questions."

"I don't have answers."

"Oh come on a man like you can't show me a good time."

"Not in here."

THE PARTY CONTINUES

"I know not here if I wanted to say meet you later. Where would I go?"

"You can't tell anyone. I'll get killed."

"I won't."

"There's a house in south beach with a purple porch-"

Gwen stood up and left the room. Brandy called it in.

David felt the cuffs slip on his wrist. He smiled as he was put in the cruiser. Thankful his sister was Brandy Hawke. He watched Brandy speed up the stairs and walk alongside Melanie.

Brandy had never seen her so pale so weak. She watched the ambulance leave they watched as crime scene documented the evidence.

"You guys might want to see this?"

They gathered around a pile of bodies in the back. Just as another officer called them to the video tapes. Brandy closed her eyes.

"Go get checked out now, Hawke."

"Ok I'll be refreshed in the morning."

"Ok."

Brandy found David at her apartment. She shouldn't have been surprised but she was. She sat down as did he.

"So how long?"

"A year."

"Melanie?"

"I needed help. I knew I could contact you through her."

"Did you hurt her?"

"Hell no sis. I had to protect her. I did protect her the others would have done far worse to her."

"Look I know the job entails a lot of things that can't be discussed. I want you to know I am going to take your word on this because we are kin. Doesn't mean that I want to punch you in the face for putting her in harm's way."

"Look I needed a way out without looking suspicious. I was deep in Brandy"

David stood as he was about to leave he spoke.

"She is one of the toughest women I know other than you. Just know she did everything she needed too to survive. I took her out of harm's way first chance I had."

David sat down he needed to come clean. Needed to tell her. She smiled looked into his eyes in recognition.

"Look whatever happened happened it can't be discussed. Probably shouldn't be discussed. Melanie means everything to me. She was there for me in a lot of rough times. Stood there right by me. Even when I didn't her I will not abandon her over anything so just go home and relax and thank you for protecting her."

Brandy watched him leave. She went and changed climbed in her car headed to find the woman of her life.

Melanie lay in utter shock. She wouldn't cry, she couldn't cry, she would do the right thing had to. Doc Tammy saw the utter shock.

"We do have procedures."

"No I won't do that."

THE PARTY CONTINUES

"Well let me know if you change your mind."

"I won't change my mind doc."

"Ok, ok your results look good. Looks like you are ok you'll be free to go in a few hours. Just try to relax. I'll get the prescriptions for the vitamins."

"Ok doc?"

Tammy turned to look at the brunette. She smiled,

"Um my girlfriend will be here soon. Can we keep this between us? I need to find a way to tell her."

"Sure Melanie. We can keep it between us."

"Thank you."

Melanie sighed in relief. She needed to find someone she trusted. Someone who would help her. She loved Brandy. They never truly discussed their intentions or possibilities. She closed her eyes and soon fell asleep.

Brandy closed her eyes as her boss told her the news. She would be going under didn't seem to be bad but with David up that meant it was her turn. She had been waiting for the opportunity to nail the bastard.

"Ok sir."

"Brandy be careful this bastard is relentless. Very skeptical right now."

"I have got it sir."

"Alright we will see you in the morning."

"Alright."

Brandy closed her eyes but knew it's probably a good thing so Melanie could recover. She saw Melanie asleep. She sat down beside Melanie and took her hand. Melanie looked in her eyes. Brandy spoke.

"You ok?"

"Yeah I'll be fine."

Brandy watched her go pale and lay down so she spoke.

"Um work has me going on leave. I'll be away for some time. I don't have a choice."

"Go home. I'll be fine. I have Sam."

"I leave in the morning."

"Ok baby. I love you."

"I love you. Are you sure you are ok?"

"Yeah so when do you get to leave?"

"Doc said a couple of hours. Why?"

"Because I have something I want to give you."

"Oh ok."

Brandy kissed her. Melanie never would get used to that feeling. She got when Brandy kissed her. Melanie smiled.

"So is it bad?"

"Yeah I won't have my phone."

"Oh so you're going under?"

Brandy nodded. Melanie watched as worry creeped on Brandy's face.

"Look we discussed this. Do what you have to just come home to me."

THE PARTY CONTINUES

She watched the smile widen on Brandy's face.

"Yes ma'am."

The doctor came in. She saw the blonde and looked in Melanie's eyes.

"Um you're ready to leave Ms. Brooks. Just make sure you take those meds as described."

"Will do doc. Thank you."

Brandy held out her hand. She helped Melanie to the door.

"Are you sure you're ok?"

"Positive just ready to get home and get recuperated."

"Heard that."

The bastard was pissed. The fucking feds were ruining his life. Took him years to build this operation and with a steady attack it has kept crumbling like dominos. He threw his cane how in the hell would he rebuild with his age. He was lucky to wake up. He chuckled as he found her hot that didn't do anything for him. It was the fear that had him go in action. He thanked god for the enhancers as he found release. He got up dressed then spoke.

"Next time be a little tighter."

He walked out of the room fixing his pants. He heard her muffled cries. He closed the door locked it. He knew that he would be alright as long as he didn't fuck up. He would make it well into old age. He dressed put on his tux and went to the door. He did have appearances to make.

Brandy lay awake that night. She held Melanie close. She could see the fading bruises knew the worst of her scars from her encounter were the ones she left unsaid and for that she knew that she had to the end the bastard's reign of terror. She held Melanie tight. She wanted to give Melanie the villa. Wanted her out of the hustle and bustle. She helped Katie out by buying and she didn't use it much anymore. Melanie would she smiled as she dozed off to sleep.

Melanie woke up with Brandy's arms around her. She smiled it wasn't often that she woke before Brandy did. So she lay there for a couple of minutes just to enjoy the feeling. She knew it would be awhile before she would feel it again. She climbed out of bed went and took her vitamins. She so wanted to tell Brandy but knew it would distract her. Brandy awoke to Melanie lost in thought.

"You ok?"

"Honey, I'm fine."

"Honey you suck at lying."

"I need to tell you something but I don't want to distract you from your job."

"Baby you can tell me anything."

Melanie at that moment wasn't so sure but she needed to see what Brandy's views were.

"When I got taken I knew that I had to do what they said I knew with them doing what they did to you. That it would be nothing for them to kill me so I-"

Brandy came to her. She saw the pain, the confusion, the tears was what grabbed her.

"I had to participate if I didn't. I didn't want to find out what would happen all. I knew was I wanted to live so I could see you again."

"And you made it."

"Yeah except-"

"Are you pregnant?"

"Yeah the doctor told me about procedures. I can't take a life Brandy. I have thought about it but I don't think that I can. I want a chance to be the parent that I never had. I want you to be part of it too. I know it is a lot to take in but I just can't take a life."

"I have always wondered what kind of a parent I would be never figured I would get the chance."

"I thought you would hate me?"

"Hate you. Hell no Melanie. I am not going to hate you for doing what you had to do to survive. I admire you for stepping up."

"So what do you say?"

"I say I was beside you before. I'll be here now."

Melanie hugged her so tight. She closed her eyes and took in this moment because she knew time was winding down.

"I'm not going to be here?"

"I know. I have got a few plans. I want someone we can trust."

"Ok baby. I do hate to say it but I do have to go."

"I know you. Be safe and come home to both of us."

"I will."

Melanie kissed her deep. Brandy plunged knowing this would be the moment that would bring her through. Brandy handed her the keys.

"Move to the villa Mels. Get out of here. I trust the people there plus Maria can help get in contact with Sam. I know she's been dying to see you. We kept her at bay till we knew you were stronger."

"Ok baby. I love you."

"I love you too."

Brandy resisted her roll her name her job. She got in the mind set as they kept briefing her she knew one slip up. She would be on the slab. She also knew that the men she was conversing with would have her back. She needed to get as close as she could get the goal was to for as high as she could take down as many as she could.

"Your Daphne Pine a runaway you joined the big amigos because it is the only family you have ever known."

"What is my trade?"

"You do what needs to be done takedown who you need to. Steal whatever to prove you belong."

"When do I ship?"

"Tonight."

"Hawke, I want this swift clean and concrete no loose ends."

She closed her eyes as she let them cut her hair. She got into her street clothes. She stood there a minute put the beanie on.

"Two things Bax."

"Keep an eye on Mels. See that Sam visits regularly please."

"Done."

"And call Katie and Harper. Tell them I want them to see to Melanie."

"Okay done?"

"Alright I am ready."

THE PARTY CONTINUES

She lay in bed knowing something needed to be done with all the assholes. She had to have something done she looked into the old man's eyes.

"Want some more?"

She needed time. Time to figure out the right move. The right time to attack. She need the information that would be the trick since he trusted no one with that kind of information but himself. She lay sexually satisfied knowing he could please her was enough for now. Soon he would be at her mercy with that thought. She smiled and dozed off.

Brandy stood on the street. She leaned against the wall. Smoking she watched the two guys come walking up the street. She stood casually smoking.

"Shouldn't be out here this time of night."

"Says who?"

"Says us this is our turf."

"It's mine now asshole."

"Not for long."

Brandy stood straight tossed her cigarette and braced herself.

"Make me move."

"You got a death wish bitch?"

"No but apparently you do."

"You know who I am?"

"I could care less who you are. I didn't start this but I will gladly end it."

"You are nothing but talk-"

That was Brandy's cue. She disarmed him and had him face down on the blacktop gun on him.

"All talk hun?"

"You the damn 5-0?"

"If I were why would I be down here wasting my fucking time fighting turf. I just practiced what I watched on television."

"You're some kind of fucking crazy."

"Now I'm going to smoke got any more issues. I will gladly resolve those as well."

"No beef here but if you need a place to hang let me know."

"I will."

Brandy watched him leave. Brandy counted to 3 timed it just right slammed his buddy on the ground fist raised. Frank saw the anger, he freaked.

"Whoa, whoa, whoa, man!"

"Fuck you!"

Brandy connected with his nose. She picked him up slung him into his buddy.

"You're a badass."

"I am not sure what to think about that."

"No all jokes aside. We could really use someone like you. The boss man is on our asses our monthly quota is short. We have a job that we need pulled and like yesterday. We could really use you on this."

THE PARTY CONTINUES

"I don't know if I can trust you. Were I come from everything comes at a cost and I am partial to my life."

"Look at least come and meet the guys and grab a bite. Think about what I said we could really use your grit on this job."

Brandy looked into his eyes for a long minute then she shrugged her shoulders and said,

"Fine, I have nothing better to do right now anyway."

Frank led Brandy down the alley to a lit house. She heard the laughter frank spoke

"They will test you. You know?"

"Naturally as I will test them."

They walked into the house. The two men she had tussled with took their jackets off. The other men stared at her. She felt the curiosity mount. She watched the biggest of them. Came to her and ask,

"Who is this Frankie boy?"

"I recruited her today."

"Oh boys, we get some fun."

Frank looked into his eyes the brute busted out laughing. Brandy knew she needed to wait. Wait for him to try to lay a hand on her and sure enough he did. Even though he was big, he was nothing but a paperweight when she tossed him over her back as she slammed him on the ground. She had her foot on his throat. She stood heard the one behind her. She spun had him by the throat and slung him against the wall. She then saw the two on either side of her. She smiled folded her hands waited for them to pounce at the same time. She slammed their heads together. She shook her head, took out a cigarette was leaning against the door jamb when Frank came to her.

"Welcome to the club. Told you, we needed you."

Brandy nodded as she lit her smoke. She exhaled as they started to moan and she heard one of them say,

"Damn Gary, get your big ass off of us."

"Where is she?"

"I wouldn't do that."

"Shut up Frankie."

Bob held the gun. Brandy spoke,

"You should listen to your friend here."

She saw the two guns. She disarmed one as she elbowed the other one in the nose. Kicked the gun away.

"Now I don't want to hurt you. I just need a place to hang my hat. I'm willing to hustle do what I have to pay my way. I really don't see this as a productive way to get your asses in the clear, do you?"

"Alright we have a job tonight on the east side."

"What kind of job?"

"Skittish?"

Brandy shot inches from his head. He could feel it, skin his hair. She saw his eyes get wide for a second.

"I don't know you tell me. See it pulls a little to the right but if I move it a few inches. Let's see if I miss?"

"Alright, alright we have caused this house it has everything just need to be vacant. Get us that house and I'll say you're in."

"By herself?"

THE PARTY CONTINUES

"Yeah."

"Whatever I thought it was going to be some real work. I didn't know I was coming on as the janitor taking out bags of bones."

"What do you plan to do?"

"Geez, now who is skittish"

"Seriously?"

"Well since to how I have done this thousands of times before the job generally calls for me to shoot her. Burry her with the bugs. Damn I'll be back in five."

Brandy shot out into the night. She looked at the picture, located the house. She went inside found the lady on the couch.

"I need you to listen to me. Very seriously. I need you to go to the police station find Chief Bax give him this and go down the street. Go now, right now."

"Okay?"

Brandy shoved her out the door and shot three rounds in the chair. She took the keys off of the table hustled into the night. Came back to the awaiting men and tossed the keys to Frank.

"All yours."

"Good work."

Brandy sat down. They stared at her, one asked,

"Why are you here?"

"Had nothing else in mind to do with my life. I'm not giving you my life story. You wanted me to clean the damn house. I did."

"Still seems odd."

"Well you learn to sharpen your skills. When you are the only one you depend on day in and day out. I have always stood alone and going through this shit. I realize why I do damn."

"True we know that don't we guys?"

Brandy lit a cigarette as they stood watching her.

"What?"

"It's just we are all on board for you joining. We do have to clear it with the bastard."

"The bastard who is that?"

"He runs the show only shows when he needs something."

"Well I mean I can help provide."

"You're a woman doll. He usually has you provide another way."

"I'm a better fighter."

Frank cleared his throat and spoke,

"We can help her guys come on. She will be better for us here. We need her skills."

"Yeah I mean you do have what we lack."

"Sure I don't feel like meeting my maker yet."

Melanie set in agony. The pain was horrible. The blood was a lot. Sam stood pacing on the phone with paramedics. David was in shock. Melanie screamed out again. The paramedics rushed in ordered everyone out of the room. Sam managed to get Doc Ruby to

THE PARTY CONTINUES

make a house call. She walked in. She saw the brunette in complete distress. She knew time was crucial. She spoke as she acted,

"Oh baby girl. I'm sorry."

"What is going on?"

"We will find out. I'm going to give you some meds it will help you relax."

"Ok."

Ruby could see the kid was completely miserable. She held the water for Melanie.

"Just breathe honey. I know it's hard but you need to try. The sooner I get you calm. The faster I can fix the problem."

"Ok."

Ruby ordered the IV. She had blood on standby. She watched as Melanie dozed.

"Ok I need people to hold her feet up. I need to get up in there."

"Ok."

Ruby took the fetus out and got all the afterbirth out. She felt the tears well up. She had to tell her. She knew how the conversation would go. She thanked everyone ushered them out. She sat as Melanie slept. Sam stood. She was already a nervous wreck. The last thing she needed to deal with was a damn chaotic man.

"Sit down!"

"I can't!"

"Listen you need to calm down for her."

"But,"

"You care for her. Don't you?"

"Of course."

"Trust me being hysterical is not the answer."

"Ok."

Katie came in. She wore the look of confusion. As Harper tried to explain what was going on. Katie put her hands on her hips. Glared at David. Harper grabbed her arm.

"Listen baby. He didn't do it."

"Well he is the only male here. Isn't he?"

"Yeah he is but…"

Katie stormed off to the door. Harper glared at David then smiled at Sam.

"Sorry love she gets like this."

"Oh it's ok. See she is not the only one emotional here. You see Mels is something special. Kind of like your Katie there so this is hard on us all but what is going to be really hard is telling her that she lost the baby."

Harper took Sam's hand. She looked into her eyes and spoke calmly.

"It's going to be hard. The shock will come first then the tears. Just be honest and do you. She trusts you. I can tell."

Sam let the tears fall as she watched Harper go out to find Katie. Harper found Katie by the truck smoking. She had to smile because Katie looked so sexy. Blonde hair waving in the wind. Katie spoke,

"You know it's been ages since I have been here. The last time I was here it was chaotic and a blur but being here now with you for Brandy. It feels different. It feels right. I would have visit Maria had I known it would have been like this. I just always thought it would be like it was when.."

"Now you know and I have to say you have made me proud."

She watched Katie look in her eyes. She saw the tears threaten but then subside. Harper took her hands. Cleared her throat,

"I honestly was prepared to go all kung fu on Bax and give him so many excuses so you wouldn't have to come but when I heard you say that you would. I was afraid it would affect you but you are handling it like a champ."

"Well when he said that Brandy asked that changed because she did save my life. The least I can is look out for Mels. What makes me mad is that Melanie sits in there in misery and there is nothing that we can do."

"Yeah there is baby. We are here for her right?"

"Yeah but nothing is going to help when she finds out that she lost the little tyke."

"Your right nothing is going to help with that but what we can do is go in there and be there for her through this."

"I know. I just don't like to see anyone in pain. Especially someone I love."

"Me either so what do you say we go rile Maria into throwing a cookout with beer. We can get Sam to invite the team. Maybe help her ease the pain a little."

"Well I will leave you to rile Maria. She can be feisty. I will go talk to Sam about the teammates."

"Sounds like a plan."

Harper pulled Katie's mouth on hers. They plunged deep then Katie pulled away.

"Not now Max. I'm in the middle of-"

"Oh come on."

Katie shot her a smile, punched her shoulder playfully then spoke.

"We get to the hotel love by all means we can."

"Now we are talking."

Sam sat with her head in her hands. She never found herself in such a nervous wreck. She heard Katie and Harper come in. Harper headed to the kitchen. Katie walked to her. She sat down beside Sam. Katie could see the worry in her face.

"So we came up with an idea. We know we can't do anything about what is going with the baby or anything but can't we have a little party. You know nothing major invite her closest friends you know people that can help us cheer her up. Harper is on Maria about the food arrangements."

At that moment they heard pans rattle and Harper come to them red faced and laughing. Sam spoke.

"Sounds like that was a trip."

"Oh yeah me and Maria have an understanding."

Sam looked back at Katie. She exhaled and stood.

"It beats what we are doing now so I say let's roll with it."

Just then the door opened. She smiled as she looked at everyone in the room. She spoke.

"She is fine just needs plenty of rest and friend's."

Harper spoke up.

"We can give her both of those things."

Ruby came to Sam and Katie. She grew more serious.

"Don't let her get to over active right now. She lost a lot of blood. I'll come back around in a few days to check on her."

"Ok doc thank you so much."

"Good call Sam. She nearly bled to death."

"I know."

"See you."

Sam came in and saw Melanie sitting there looking at her hands. Sam could see the evidence where she had been crying. It really tore at her heart. Sam sat down just as Katie and harper came in.

"What did I do wrong?"

"Honey you did absolutely nothing wrong?"

"Yeah Mels you did everything right."

"Then why did this have to happen to me? To my baby?"

Sam spoke she stood as she cleared her throat. Looked Melanie in the eyes.

"Things happen Melanie and the sad thing about it is sometimes there is no explanation. What I can tell you from experience is it is best to not dwell on that because if you do it will eat you alive."

Harper came to Melanie's other side. Melanie looked at Harper. Harper sat down. She wiped her eyebrow.

> "So me and Katie. We kind of made plans to help you with this because to be honest all of us feel helpless. We kind of set things in motion for a small gathering of your closest friends."

Katie spoke up.

> "Yeah because maybe one of your friend's moms went through something. They can help or maybe it will do what we want it to and help you forget this for a few minutes at a time."

Melanie looked at the three women. Who stood in her room at that moment she knew what Brandy meant when she said that friends can be more than family then actual family. Sam took her hand as the other two came close.

> "We will help you get through this Melanie. You are not alone in this."

> "Thank you guys so much. I mean I feel really horrible right now but just knowing that I have you guys with me. Helps out a lot and I love the idea of the gathering. Thank you guys."

Sam spoke as she looked at the other three.

> "Doc said rest so we figured if we could somehow get you in the family room then there would be plenty of room for everyone."

Melanie smiled at her friends wishing for the one person who she knew couldn't be there. The one person she knew who would make

THE PARTY CONTINUES

her feel better with just a hug. She closed her eyes hoping that wherever she was at she was safe.

Brandy found herself in a sticky situation. She had sent the boys out to scavenge now. She had a prowler lurking around so she went high. She saw the woman run out into the night. Luckily she had them build the storage underground. She sat there til she saw the men come up through the woods. She had to commend them on the quietness more than she could say for their recent visitor. She slid out of the tree and on the roof.

"Where is she?"

Brandy dropped in behind them.

"We had a visitor."

"A visitor?"

"Yeah some chick snooping around took off like a bat out of hell."

"Gwen she's hauling messages to him. He will show soon."

"Good right now we need to keep our shit low."

"He will want something?"

"Okay you have gotten us this far. We trust you."

"Okay I cased a high end jeweler. He is loaded. The take is plenty enough for him. Some for us we will hit at first light."

"Won't there be cops?"

"Not at first light. Shift change told you I did my homework plus tomorrow morning they are moving diamonds."

"Risky?"

"Scared Bob?"

"No just…"

"Look if I do most of the work. I know you will kill me split the profits. I'm not stupid Frankie. You said you needed to make up the loss. This is way risky or not there is more at stake than just a couple bullets flying if we don't have his cut when he shows up."

"Fine, I'm in."

"Me too"

"Us too bob?"

"I don't know"

Brandy knew it was her chance to prove herself. She came to him.

"How did you make it this far?"

"I don't know."

"You don't provide. You're out that's that."

"That is not fair."

Brandy pulled the gun out cocked it.

"Like I said you don't provide you're out."

"You won't shoot me."

Brandy hit him in the arm. Watched him fall. She heard dead silence. She spoke her voice cold her point clear.

"Now if we are done. I have got a plan to perfect so we come out clean."

THE PARTY CONTINUES

The men set still. It was at that moment she had earned their respect. She got looking at the floor plans. Frank came to her as did the others.

"They will be taking the diamonds out back in the alley. There is only one camera. Frank take it out. Gary you're on detail. See the huggers let out the signal that leaves me and Hank. There should only be two guards and two officers. Frank when you get the camera done take out the officer. We will meet back here after I ditch the truck."

"Alright."

Brandy watched as the sun rose. She prepped herself for this battle. Knew this battle would be the one to get her higher in ranks. She needed that. She smiled as she led them out. She knew what had to be done just then she watched as a group showed up. She heard frank say,

"That's them."

"So where are we headed?"

"Out to collect."

"Gwen says it's bare in there like always."

"She's lying, go look."

Brandy watched him go in the house come back out with a smile on his face.

"That's what I like success."

"I swear."

"Shut up I'll deal with you later. In fact why don't you join them? See how the real world works for a change."

"No baby."

"Shut up. I was just about ready to cash you in anyway."

Brandy watched him grab her by the hair of the head and drag her behind him. She closed her eyes. His brutality had to stop. She had to get close but knew she couldn't blow her cover.

"Come on boys our window is slimming."

He watched them go through the woods. He loved success just wasn't used to it. Brandy eased them in she sent them in motion just as Bax and the crew came out of hiding.

"Not this time Daphne."

"Fuck! Can't you leave me alone for 5 minutes?"

"Officers are killed you're here. Looks like you did it."

"Whoa!!!!!!!!"

Brandy closed her eyes as she sat with her head down. Frankie watched her get wheeled away then felt the cuffs on him as well.

"Whoa we didn't do this?"

"Right?"

Brandy was fuming when she went to the police department. She was led inti the interrogation room. Baxter came in.

"What the hell is going on?"

"We had to pull you up."

"Why?"

"Do you know a Grace Short?"

"Grace yeah I know her why?"

THE PARTY CONTINUES

"She was the woman casing your place last night. The meeting this morning was her as well."

"So she didn't make me?"

"Not yet. I can't have you out there. I can't risk it."

"I was so close."

"I know. We have another officer taking over."

"Damn it Baxter. This is my case!"

"Sorry, Hawke. Melanie would kill me if I let you die."

Brandy glared at him. She knew he was right still didn't make it any easier. She sat down closed her eyes.

"Just rest, Hawke. I'll drive you home here in a bit."

Melanie stood on the court. George knew he would find her. There he watched as she shot the jumper.

"So one more game?"

"Yeah I'm sorry. I haven't been here."

"Oh child it is fine. I know they were legitimate reasons."

"Yeah I still feel awful."

"Ah it is nothing. Life happens Melanie just know I am sure glad to have you back and that you are healthy enough to play."

"Oh trust me. I am grateful that I still can play the game. I love for the team I love."

"Good now go rest up for the game."

"Ok see you around five thirty."

Melanie came out and seen Sam waiting by her car. She had to smile. Sam had become her rock through the last several months. Melanie walked up to her.

"Well good to see you crazy girl but um I thought your car was over there?"

"Oh it is silly but Baxter called."

"He did?"

"Yeah."

"What did he want?"

"You will see."

Melanie arched a brow. She knew it had to be about Brandy. She felt the butterflies well up in her stomach. Sam drove in silence.

"Don't worry Mels. I'm sure everything is ok."

"Yeah but he doesn't call like this."

"Does so he just called yesterday."

"Sam I am serious. I'm worried."

"Don't worry. Everything is fine."

Melanie looked at her hands. She didn't know how Brandy would react to her losing the baby. She just didn't know anything. Brandy had been under for some time. She would soon find out as Sam pulled up into the precinct parking lot.

Baxter knew if anyone could calm Brandy down it would be Mels. She was their only hope. He watched as Melanie walked in. She held the look of confusion Baxter knew he had to explain things to her.

"Come with me Melanie please."

THE PARTY CONTINUES

Melanie followed Baxter to his office. He shut the door, cleared his throat as she watched him sit.

"Relax she is fine. I just had to intervene. I had to bring her up earlier than anticipated. She is pissed but I got information that told me her life was in danger under. I need you to try to talk to her."

"You want me to talk to her about this?"

"I just need you to do you Melanie. I just wanted you to know what was going on."

"I can try but we both know. She probably will just get mad at me."

"We have to try Mels."

Sam spoke as she winked.

"Don't worry Mels. My couch is available."

Melanie shot her a look then followed Baxter, Melanie took a deep breath and walked in. She saw Brandy all dirty. Her clothes were ragged, her hair was a shag. Brandy looked into her eyes.

"Why are you here?"

"I don't know Brandy you tell me?"

Brandy glared at her. Wiped a hand on her brow.

"I'm just pissed."

"Oh I know you're pissed because Baxter saved your life. You're pissed because you didn't make that beg break. Grow up Brandy life throws you curves, you just learned to take the good with the bad."

Brandy stood, got in her face.

> "Grow up. Hell lady I have been busting my ass out there while you have been doing nothing but sitting on your ass so don't tell me anything about growing up."

Melanie held her hand to stop them from coming in. Her voice broke but the tears did not fall she cleared her throat.

> "Your right I have been doing nothing but let me tell you something when you walk out of here find the woman I fell in love with first because this is not the woman I fell in love with."

> "Look."

> "Your right I don't understand."

Melanie walked out the door passed Gwen and Baxter. She locked eyes with Sam who followed her out the door to the car and home.

> "She was so angry, so scary."

> "Yeah I saw that."

> "Sam after the game tonight. Will you take a trip with me?"

> "Well I'm sure after what happened Baxter won't mind or Gwen but sure."

> "Ok thank you."

The game was a blur all she knew was that they won. She closed her eyes as she finally let that breath out. She was holding deep down inside. She tried to not think about the hurt that still lingered. She knew that whatever Brandy was going through must be bad for her to be so angry. She sighed grabbed her bag knew she needed her friends. Melanie smiled when she found Sam walking to the door.

> "Look who gets to go on a road trip with the MVP."

THE PARTY CONTINUES

Melanie smiled as she gave Sam a hug. She threw her gym bag in the back of the car. She needed to be away for a while. Needed to be back home just to recoup and rethink.

Brandy ran a hand over her face. What did she do? She didn't have anything to apologize for. She was out grinding but deep down. She knew Melanie hadn't sat that got her thinking where the baby was. She hadn't looked pregnant. She closed her eyes. She called Gwen.

"What?"

"Can we talk?"

"Talk."

"Seriously Gwen."

"Seriously talk."

"Tell me what happened to Mels while I was gone."

"Nope that is her story to tell."

"I want to know."

"Well maybe you should have thought about that Hawke before you screamed in her face."

"I didn't scream."

"Didn't you?"

"I just was mad."

"Look if I where Mels I would tell you to kiss my ass. I am not if I know Melanie which I did you hurt her bad Hawke. Whatever you do you better be on your knees asking forgiveness."

"But I didn't do anything."

"Just remember that."

Brandy sighed as she heard the click. She didn't understand why she was painted the bad guy. Didn't anyone understand she was so close she could have put the cuffs on him? She was about to punch the wall when she heard the knock on her door. She took a deep breath as she saw David standing there. She opened the door David stormed in right a passed her and began pacing. She could tell his was mad.

"Sis?"

"What?"

"Tell me it is not true?"

"Tell you what is not true?"

"Did you yell at Melanie?"

"Yeah I was pissed. I actually was in what is going on what is so…"

"I respect you and I love you but you best apologize."

"Again with me saying sorry doesn't anyone understand my side?"

"Yeah so?"

"Would you be so fucking cocky if you had got pulled out and Melanie was dead?"

"What?"

"Exactly you have been so focused on you. You haven't even noticed anything else."

"What happened?"

"That is Melanie's story to tell if she chooses you should know. I leave her the pleasure of making you feel like an ass."

THE PARTY CONTINUES

David left Brandy felt the weight of guilt hang on her shoulders. This time when she closed her eyes she didn't see rage. David was right she had already felt like an ass. She called Gwen back

"Look Hawke."

"Gwen?"

"Oh."

"Where is she?"

"What makes you think I know?"

"Because I asked you and Sam to look out for her."

"Brandy I don't know. I swear."

"Yeah right."

"Honest hon I don't if I did I would tell you."

"I fucked up."

"Yeah blondie this time you really did."

"I got to fix it."

"Call Sam."

Brandy ran a hand over her brow as she nodded and dialed Sam's number. She wasn't surprised when she got the voicemail. She just left a message to call her back. She could not sit around. She needed to find her then it hit her. She grabbed her bag and her keys.

Melanie sat on the bank on Katie's farm. She watched as the river ran slowly. She loved the solitude. She could think out here amongst the trees and water. She smiled as Sam handed her the water.

"Brandy called."

"Oh did you pick it up?"

"No but she wants me to call her back."

"Do what you think is best Sam. I'm not ready to deal with that conversation."

They both turned to the red truck that pulled up. Katie jumped out and hugged Melanie and Sam as she spoke.

"I got your message. What is going on Mels?"

"It's Brandy."

Harper came up behind Katie. She cleared her throat.

"So why don't we go back to the farm and discuss this."

"Oh honey there is no skunks out here."

"Still you never know and I don't want to find out. I'll buy you a beer."

Melanie smiled as she stood locked eyes with Sam. Who was already saying hell yeah! Melanie knew that with her friends she would figure out just what she needed to do. She sat around the camp fire as Katie passed out the beer. She sat beside Katie.

"So what is going on?"

"It's just what Brandy said that hurt worse than anything she could do."

"What was that?"

"She was pissed that Baxter had to pull her up. He wanted me to try to calm her down well I tried without prevail. She got in my face and told me I didn't do anything but sit because I told her that life happens and she needed to grow up."

THE PARTY CONTINUES

Harper stood Katie jumped up.

"Look here Red that's not going to solve the issue."

"No but we are all thinking it."

Harper looked at Sam and Melanie who both smiled. Harper flung her hands up as she grabbed a beer. Melanie closed her eyes just then Katie's phone rang. She watched Brandy's face pop up. She shot Melanie a look then answered it.

"Hey Hawke."

"I need help."

"Sounds familiar."

"Look I need to know if she is ok."

"How should I know Brandy and if I did do you think I would tell you after what you did?"

"I was hoping I need to fix it Katie."

"Yeah you better."

"I will be there in a few days."

"Play."

Katie ran a hand down her face as she sat down again. Harper came over with the plate full of food. She looked in Katie's eyes.

"You know I have respect for Hawke because she saved your life and mine. You also know what I think of assholes."

"Easy baby I agree I do the thing that bothers me is Brandy normally can compartmentalize."

"She was under really deep."

"I know Mels. The thing is when I met her she was deep. I actually thought she was one of the men that grabbed me. She came out fine."

"She said she was close to nailing the bastard."

"Oh I get it."

Harper spoke up took a swig of her beer as she smiled.

"Well she is going to eat a lot of crow when she comes."

"Yeah I agree a lot."

Melanie stood locked eyes with Sam. She spoke.

"I don't want to be here."

"Listen love. I know she is the last person you want to see right now but you need to give her a chance."

"I'm done being hurt."

Katie smiled as she walked to Melanie.

"Yeah I have been there it works for a while but in the end you will still need her."

"Yeah well I'm not going to make it easy for her."

"Who said make it easy Mels. Hell no don't make it easy just hear her out."

Brandy hoped she would find Melanie. Set things straight how could she have been so selfish all she knew was Melanie Brooks had to be in her life. She knew the minute she met Melanie. No one can deny that feeling. She didn't believe in love before Melanie. She was positive it wouldn't be any better after Melanie. She had practice several ways to grovel but doubted it would help her case with Melanie so she would do the best thing she had be honest and hope Melanie would

THE PARTY CONTINUES

find it in her heart to forgive her. As Brandy hit Fleming County she felt the guilt get heavier as the pit of her stomach got even more uneasy. It had been a while since she had seen Katie. She sure wished it was under better circumstances. She knew Mels had come home she also knew if she didn't do anything. She would never be satisfied. She pulled into Katie's driveway. She climbed out expecting Katie all smiles. She found Harper's arms folded.

"What is going on?"

"That is what I want to know."

Brandy locked eyes with Melanie odd she felt relief and regret all at once. Brandy put her hands in her jeans, her blonde locks flew in the wind. She stopped in front of Melanie at that moment. She knew she would cry but held back.

> "I'm sorry. I was selfish and self-centered for a second there. I believe I had the god complex. I'm truly sorry the one thing I know for sure is I can't lose you if you can find it in your heart please forgive me."

> "Brandy I didn't like what I saw. How you treated me I understand you were under a while but to be so hateful to me hell no."

> "Just tell me what went on please are you alright?"

Melanie looked at Sam, Katie and Harper. They nodded all had their arms folded. She bit back a smile. She loved the way Brandy cared for her. It was sincere. She was so glad. She had a family behind her now too. That made her happy.

> "I am now. Played my first game a week ago."

> "The baby?"

> "I miscarried. It was horrible. Sam, Katie and Harper helped me. What hurt the most Brandy is I wished you were there with me. Just to hold my hand, tell me

things were going to be alright then soon as I see you that is what I got. Can I forgive you? I did that the minute you did it to me. It is the hurt I can't shake."

"I'm so sorry but that explains why David nearly took my head off."

"He was there so was Gwen."

"They wouldn't tell me. Gwen wants me to grovel."

"No to the grovel Hawke. Just give me sometime"

Brandy knew to get her. She had to abide by what was requested of her. Even if she knew it would hurt. She stood with her hands in her pockets.

"I do wish that I was there for you."

"Do you because when I went in to that interrogation room. I saw a side of you that I never saw before. A side of you that honestly scared me and that woman didn't want anything to do with me or my baby."

"I was in the moment dammit."

Harper spoke up. Stood up looked in Brandy's eyes.

"I understand it is grueling Hawke. I respect that. I respect you because you protected my wife however me seeing your fiancée deathly white. Her bleeding profusely and whaling in agony has me standing here and now telling you that you want to talk but you will not be yelling at her not in my presence."

Melanie watched Brandy go to her car and back out. Sam came up behind her. Melanie closed her eyes as Sam put a protective arm on Melanie's shoulder.

"Hey you okay?"

THE PARTY CONTINUES

"I will survive."

"Come on we need to get back. George has been blowing my phone up wondering if we are going to be back for the scrimmage."

Melanie turned and went to Katie and Harper. She hugged Harper tight and looked into her eyes.

"Thanks Harper that truly meant a lot."

"Anytime Mels."

She went to Katie hugged her. Katie held on a little longer. Melanie pulled away as she did she spoke.

"Just so the both of you know. I now consider you my family. I have never had that. I truly do thank the both of you for being there for me and helping me with Brandy."

Katie spoke as she lit a cigarette.

"Melanie we consider you family too and family is always there for family. You need us, you just call and we will be there."

"Well work calls. We need to get back."

"Yeah make sure you crush those tigers now."

Melanie sent a smile Harper's way as they climbed in the car and Sam sent it in motion. Melanie oddly felt good sure. She knew she should feel sad and in a way she did but she felt complete.

Sam spoke as she cleared her throat.

"So I'm heading to the condo Mels."

"So head to the condo Sam. I need a minute of solitude anyway."

"So what's going on Sam? You only head to the condo when Gwen falls short."

"So my neighbor aka aunt tells me she saw Gwen on the arm of a red head even sent a photo."

"I'm sorry Sam."

"Anyway I think we need a drink and just some down time."

"Yeah we do."

"Listen Melanie I don't know if it is the right time to tell you but I do need to tell you one thing. I don't agree with what Brandy is doing. Especially after what you have been through."

"Well right now I don't want to talk about it. I know you wouldn't because you were there and you were right beside me."

"Well I do have my moments. I would never treat you like that."

"I know. I also know she was in the middle of a job and probably got side winded. I get it still doesn't take away the hurt."

"No excuse Melanie. I'm sorry."

Brandy sat at the bar with Gwen. She sat watching Gwen eyeing women. She shook her head.

"You have Sam, Gwen."

"No harm in looking."

"Look if that is the game I am out. You should get home before you do something that you will regret. Yeah it is fun but Gwen Samantha is the best."

Brandy finished her draft and walked to the door. She noticed Gwen on the red heads lap. She shook her head and went to her car as she went to her apartment. She thought of Melanie in that pinstripe suit. She smiled as she let herself in her apartment. She knew she needed to give Melanie space but why did she feel like she should just rush over and beg and plead. Why did it have to hurt so damn bad? She lay on the couch and clicked the tv on. She saw her gramps number on her phone. She closed her eyes.

"Yeah?"

"Princess, how are you doing?"

"Don't pretend, this is a social call pap."

"Oh it is a social call to where I ream your ass for allowing the best thing that came into your life leave."

"She said she wanted space."

"Damn say that princess what she really wants is for you to show her just how much you mean to her."

"Well I highly doubt that gramps. Since to how I was practically escorted to my car."

"Think what you want princess but at least think about what I said."

Brandy heard the click. She called Melanie praying that she would answer.

"What?"

"Please can I get a chance to make it up to you?"

"You know Hawke. I never had much but I do have common decency. I didn't have to go anywhere to be over looked unless I'm needed. I agreed to go with you that day because I sincerely thought you wanted me as I wanted you. It kills me because as much as I want to hate you. I can't. I love you and you always seem to show me just how much you don't love me. It's okay it will take time for me to get over the fact that I'm just not good enough for you but I'm resilient remember."

Brandy had told her that the other night. She closed her eyes. She deserved that last remark. She knew that she needed work. Baxter had given her leave for being heated over the pull up. She called him.

"You."

"Hey Hawke. What's up?"

"Everything nothing I need to come back. I fucked things up with Melanie if i don't come back it might be permanent."

"Good I'll see you tomorrow morning."

Brandy sat at her desk just grateful for the work. The file on her desk sat untouched as she couldn't get Melanie out of her mind. Who was she kidding? She knew she had done wrong. She also knew to get Melanie back she would have to give her space and time so she took a deep breath set out on her first file. Baxter peeked in.

"You ok?"

"I will be."

Baxter came in. Closed the door sat down in front of Brandy.

"When I first met Sam. I was blew away by her skill."

"If this is a preaching you can keep it."

"No just listen. She blew me away seriously my heart hit the ground so I made a play. She agreed it was wonderful hot then she sat me down. We had a talk. She loved me wanted me in her life but she loved someone else."

THE PARTY CONTINUES

"That was cold."

"Not really not when the other person is your partner."

"Gwen?"

"I was pissed. Hurt nearly, fired Gwen over it. See Brandy she was honest with me. I still get to see my girls. We have family gatherings. I see it with you. I see it with Melanie. It's there, everything will be ok."

"How can you know she is hurt? I hurt her bad"

"Yeah you did but you see the error of your ways. Most don't."

"It hurts so bad Bax."

"Well take that and help me solve this case."

"Bradford?"

"No he's been quiet."

"Too quiet."

"Yeah the case now is in the conference room."

"Ok I will. Thanks."

"Anytime."

Brandy followed Baxter to the conference room. She saw the photos of the women.

"This perp likes to abduct these women. Keeps them roughly a week then they end up like this."

"Where?"

"Colorado.'

Brandy looked at him.

"Colorado?"

"Yeah someone let it loose. We have a top notch detective. They want our eyes."

Brandy sipped her coffee. She studied the pictures the women seemed upper middle class til the last one.

"What happened? What made him change from upper middle class to her?"

"Maybe victim by chance."

"Nah something happened between the times with the last victim to her."

He stood above the bitch. She costed him his prize target. She costed him his business. The last thing he need was the greedy fucking feds knocking on his door. He didn't have time to save face and play nice. Oh he was so fucking pissed. He slammed her again. Heard her cry out. She was no good to him now no good at all. He would have to knock her off. He would have fun first he knew she would do anything he asked so he professed his apologies and he smiled as she did exactly what he wanted. Let the sensation run through him as he felt himself release. He zipped his pants and lit a cigarette. He smiled as she never moved, he kicked her feet out from under her as her lifeless body fell to the floor. He cursed.

"No damn it."

He liked taking their life feeling that moment when it was over. She robbed him of that. He sat at the table deciding what he would do. She wasn't one of his normal picks. Hell even her death wasn't his way. He want ready for the feds to be knocking so he dragged her body to the woods behind his house and buried her body after he was done with that. He went and sat at the table. He knew the big bastard would call soon since she was dead. He would play it off as he usually did. Sure enough his phone rang.

THE PARTY CONTINUES

"Yo."

"So where's Gwen?"

"I haven't seen her since the feds picked her up."

"Is that so?"

"That is so that little job costed me some good men."

"Listen to me you little twerp. This comes back to me I will have your head. Gwen was my favorite."

"Like I said I haven't seen her as far as I know you are clean."

"Better be."

Bradford smiled as he exhaled on his cig.

"I want this chick."

Bradford saw the brunette. He immediately recognized her. Felt fear creep up his spine.

"Problems?"

"No."

"Good you have a week."

Bradford heard the click.

"Bastard is sicker than I am."

He looked at the photo again. Sure he would want me to go right into the feds and grab her. He muttered asshole as he stood up shook off the frustration as he began mapping out his plan. He really didn't like the plan and knew if he followed through with it. He would be caught knew if he didn't he would be dead. He didn't know what to do. Truth be told he had been tired for a while. He grinned that grin he knew what he would do.

Brandy stood at the crime scene wasn't as brutal as some but still she knew that the bastard wasn't done.

"You ok, Hawke?"

"Yeah just something is off."

"What do you mean easiest case we ever caught?"

"Too easy."

"Exactly points for the blonde so smart yet so stupid."

Brandy watched him point a gun at Gwen's head ease her out the door.

"Anyone follows I will kill her after I have fun."

Brandy watched as he led Gwen to the awaiting car.

"Damn it."

"We will get her back."

"Damn it Bax. I know that just it's how she will come back. I worry about."

Brandy called Skylar.

"APB on black mercury sedan license alfa-delta-charlie-4-6-9."

"Tracking now headed east on Beltway."

Brandy hurried to the cruiser. Baxter on her heels.

"Keep talking Sky."

"Uh he is still on Beltway."

Brandy weaved through the traffic. She saw him weaving through the vehicles.

"Ok Sky. I see him."

Baxter too the phone.

"Sky notify any departments out this way. Tell them to be on standby. Oh and Sky. He has Gwen."

"Oh on it sir."

Brandy eased right on his bumper. She looked at Bax as the van stopped. They stopped a few feet away. Brandy climbed out, gun cocked.

"Let me see your hands."

Brandy eased to the driver's door and cursed as she didn't see a body then she saw it.

"Get back now."

She followed Baxter back to the car. She hit reverse blocked the cars off. Baxter called the bomb squad.

"What the hell?"

At that moment they heard the explosion. Brandy hung her head then Bax's phone rang.

"Hello."

"Like that chief?"

"Not impressed."

"Listen I won't hurt your precious agent but have to do something for me."

"What would that be? I do need a proof of life."

"I'm ok Bax. See now back to what I was saying. She gets returned if you do something for me."

"What?"

"I want a helicopter and a passport."

"Ok where do I send it?"

"At the abandoned factory."

"Alright."

Baxter locked eyes with Brandy as he made the call.

"Skylar get the eyes in the sky at the old mill works have one unmarked."

"Yes sir."

Brandy drove to the old factory. She heard the helicopters. They climbed out.

"Ok your ride is coming, send her out."

Brandy watched Gwen run out behind Baxter. Gwen was unharmed. They watched him climb the ladder to the helicopter and the message that they apprehended him. Gwen gave Baxter a hug then looked into his eyes. Bax spoke.

"You ok?"

"I will be."

They headed to the precinct. Brandy sighed with relief until they heard the distress signal.

"Skylar?"

"Umm were clear subjects in the interrogation room."

"Then what is going on?"

"I will find out."

Brandy pulled up and rushed inside. They saw him with his gun on Skylar.

"Look I'm going to die anyway whether it's by your gun or not."

"So why not help u?"

"You people never helped me."

"You never let us."

"Bullshit all those times you all came to the house and the bitch would say oh she just fell on his skateboard or he got in to a fight at school. You never saw the truth."

"I wasn't the chief then."

"It's still the same system."

"Yeah it's the same system different rules. I'm sorry. I wasn't chief. I would have helped."

"Yeah right."

"Seriously."

"I don't by that shit."

"You don't have too. I have plenty of kids who would say you are wrong."

Skylar found her moment disarmed him as Gwen arrested him. Brandy spoke.

"Somebody is his boss."

"Yeah and my guess a powerful man."

Melanie sat in her car. She hadn't seen Brandy since they met in Kentucky. The truth was she missed her like crazy. Wanted to be with her. She watched as she headed to her car. Melanie pulled out behind her and followed her to her apartment. Melanie smiled as Brandy climbed out and looked her way. Melanie couldn't deny the feelings that were awakening. She climbed out as Brandy came her way. Brandy wanted to think that she was dreaming when she saw her in her review now all she wanted to do was pull Melanie into a hug and hold her tight. That was exactly what she did. Melanie closed her eyes.

"I so wanted to make this big speech but I forget everything when I'm around you."

Melanie watched as Brandy wiped her eyes. She pulled Brandy to her. Took her lips. They got lost in a taste that both missed. Melanie pulled away.

"I didn't come for an apology. Hawke. I came for my woman is she still available?"

"Oh hell yeah she is."

"Good then lead me in so I can finish the rest of my plans."

"Yes ma'am!"

Brandy wasn't sure if she'd get Melanie back but now that she did she knew she was the most blessed woman on earth and owed Mels everything she had for giving her another chance she watched as Mels slept beside her so calm and siren she heard her phone buzz to life she sure hoped that it wasnt Baxter calling her in she picked her phone up hoping to see any number but the one that meant she would leave Melanie she smiled as she saw Katie's number she answered with a sigh of relief

"hey"

"Hey hawke call at a bad time?"

"Oh no what's up?"

"Oh nothing just Harper got herself in a bind"

THE PARTY CONTINUES

Automatically the cop in Brandy was ready she paused as she asked

"What kind of bind?"

"Chill Hawke not that kind of bind geez all you cops think alike no no she just needs Mels to help her out"

"with what?"

"Well she spoke up to her super about how she knew Red Hot and now he threw her under the bus with the little tykes basketball tournement"

"oh so what does she need Mels for?"

"see she is playing against the local firemen and lets just say its a big rivalry"

"oh so when do y'all need her?"

"well since to how the tournament is in three weeks as soon as possible"

"i'll tell her

"i'll do it"

Brandy heard the groggy voice beside her Brandy looked into her eyes

"you sure?"

"Definitely they were there when i was in my toughest times hell yeah i will help red with this basketball tournament that is what family is for isn't it?"

"that is what family is for baby Katie she says she is on board"

"hell yeah we got this in the bag see y'all soon"

"definitely we will leave out tomorrow evening"

"Good"

Brandy hung up the phone pulled Melanie to her words wasn't nessecary not at this moment all that was needed was the two hearts that were beating Melanie broke the silence

> "you ok?"

> "never better"

> "will you be able to go with me?"

> "oh most definitely i just came up so i have time enough"

> "good"

Melanie was standing in front of twelve screaming girls she couldn't help but smile as they came jumping around her she remembered being twelve and knew she was meant to be here harper broke her train of thought

> "ok girls now we know the firemen are desperate creatures and have the cup well we are getting it back this year because my friend Red Hot is going to help us out now what i need you to do today is listen to her and let her teach you a few things that will help us win that cup who is with me?"

They all cheered Harper walked toward Melanie who smiled

> "i hope you don't mind but i brought back up"

Harper saw the whole Flames team walk out on the court sam walked up to Melanie

> "told you we would show we are a team and we stick together"

THE PARTY CONTINUES

Harper stood shocked Melanie and Sam shook their heads as they began to assemble the kids in groups by the time the first practice was over both were tired and very optimistic about their chances

Harper stood in the middle of the court in a heated discussion with Brandy Katie Sam and Melanie stood back and watched as both women were red faced and nose to nose Katie looked at Melanie

> "Do you know what this is about?"
>
> "i know what you know"
>
> "Well the game starts in an hour and we need to warm up"
>
> "i know"

About that time both women came to the group in smiles and slapping each other on the back they especially chuckeled when they saw the looks of confusion on the women Katie cleared her throat and Melanie locked eyes with Brandy and saw the humor Harper blasted

> "Well Hawke looks like we succeeded they actually think we were in an argument"
>
> "i know easy baby i was just getting Red over there in the mood to argue with the ref"

Melanie had to chuckle then following suit the whole group was laughing they were interrupted when the girls came charging the court Melanie knew it was time to get ready to make the charge to victory she followed harper to the center of the court

> "all right girls you have worked for this now is the time to shine"
>
> "That's right now is the time that all of those practices pay off remember what we taught you"

"Coach Harper?"

"Yes Windy"

"i'm nervous"

Melanie remembered her first game she smiled and went to the girl melanie cleared her throat and began the same speech that joe had told her

> "you are now yes but when you get out on the floor for the game block out everything but what you know when that whisltle blows remember the lessons and let instinct kick in you will do great"

She watched as the young lady soaked up her information and nodded in understanding about that time the other team came out on the floor Harper nodded in approval and ushered her team on the sidelines she quickly found Sam and Melanie

"Ooh boy they lost to this team?"

"i know fundamentals are lacking"

"i'll have you know they had better players last year"

Melanie turned to Harper she saw the worried look Harper arched a brow

"Whats the problem Mels?"

"you knew they sucked didnt you?"

"Well maybe"

"seriously?"

"Well no i didnt til yesterday when i stumbled on them out here"

"Whats the real reason you had me come out here?"

THE PARTY CONTINUES

About that time the whistle blew taking their attention to the center of the court both women walked out to the ref

> "ok ladies we want a good clean game and since you Ms. Harper are the vistor y'all are the visiting team
>
> "good i crush on the road we will take tails"

They watched the ref nod and flip the coin Melanie watched the coin fall with tails on top she cheered the man smirked she smiled and wished him luck as she jogged off the court she went to windy

> "Ok Dimes listen to me number two is fast but lacks the handles swipe when you see the opportunity don't hesitate to shoot if you feel it"
>
> "ok coach"

Melanie let out the breath she realized she was holding as she watched the game go under way she wanted windy to do great she watched as number two did a fancy two step and windy swipe the ball and she passed it to laura who laid it in she cheered

> "way to go windy!"

By the time the game was over it wasn't a contest the Policemen won by a landslide the girls held up the cup of marbles as if it was the championship she locked eyes with Brandy and then spoke

> "ok so we won the marbles now i want to tell you what your real trophy is"

Everyone got silent and stared at melanie who was smiling from ear to ear

> "what?"
>
> "since you won the game and showed that you actually are committed i am inviting you all to join the flames boot camp and mentorship program"
>
> "Really?"

Melanie locked eyes with windy she held back the tears as she nodded Windy ran up and hugged her so hard

"Thanks coach"

After the pizza and ice cream the girls went home Melanie hadn't forgot the conversation she had with Harper she found the very woman in conversation with Brandy this time it was serious Melanie walked up

"ok i live with a cop whats going on?"

Both women turned as if they were caught with their hand in the cookie jar Harper stuttered Brandy spoke

"i dont keep secrets Harper"

"Fine i was telling Brandy here my secret to catching the perfect catfish"

"Really??"

"Honest

At that moment in time sam had came out the house in tears she dropped the phone where she stood and slumped on the steps head in her hands immediately the women rushed to her side

"Crazy Lady what's going on?"

Sam couldn't talk she couldn't find the words how was she going to explain anything about that phone call who would understand Who would understand how she felt at this moment and how horrible it is to get the information she just got she spoke

"their gone!"

"Who is gone"

"My aunt and uncle"

THE PARTY CONTINUES

Everyone locked eyes knowing that it was going to be hell getting anything out of her they ushered in the house hoping to calm her down long enough to get answers Melanie closed her eyes she didn't know the pain of loss but she knew the idea she knew that if she lost anyone in the room at that moment she would be hysterical and she knew she was grateful for the small family she had been blessed with and knew with them she would be ok

www.ingramcontent.com/pod-product-compliance
Lightning Source LLC
Chambersburg PA
CBHW021440070526
44577CB00002B/226